EASY & ELEGANT ENTREES

Other titles in the *Healthy Selects* Series:

Great Starts & Fine Finishes
Savory Soups & Salads
Quick & Hearty Main Dishes
Simple & Tasty Side Dishes

EASY & ELEGANT ENTREES

Frank R. Blenn

 American Diabetes Association.

| *Publisher* | *Editorial Director* | *Managing Editor* |
| Susan H. Lau | Peter Banks | Christine Welch |

Assistant Managing Editor
Laurie Guffey

Associate Editor
Sherrye Landrum

Printed in the United States of America
99 98 97 96 95 94   10 9 8 7 6 5 4 3 2 1

American Diabetes Association
1660 Duke Street
Alexandria, VA 22314

Page design and typesetting services by Insight Graphics, Inc.
Cover design by Wickham & Associates, Inc.

Library of Congress Cataloging-in-Publication Data

Blenn, Frank R., 1963-
Easy & elegant entrees / Frank R. Blenn.
p. cm. — (Healthy selects)
Includes index.
ISBN 0-945448-40-6 (pbk.) : $8.95
1. Diabetes—Diet therapy—Recipes. 2. Entrées (Cookery)
I. Title. II. Title: Easy and elegant entrees. III. Series.
RC662.B595 1994
641.8'2—dc20   94-36830 CIP

CONTENTS

FOREWORD

The American Diabetes Association is proud to announce *Healthy Selects,* a new cookbook series dedicated to the premise that light, healthy food can be good for you *and* taste great, too. *Easy & Elegant Entrees,* the second book in the series, is a collection of easy-to-prepare main dish recipes you can serve at elegant parties or comfortable family dinners. Each recipe has American Diabetes Association-approved exchanges and all nutritional information provided. We know you'll enjoy the new ways to serve some of your favorite foods, as well as the unique ideas found in the series.

Author Frank Blenn created these recipes to help others cope with diabetes, and thought to offer them to us in an effort to reach and assist a wider audience. We deeply appreciate his generosity. The Association also owes a special debt of gratitude to Madelyn L. Wheeler, MS, RD, CDE, and her company, Nutritional Computing Concepts, for the thorough and careful preparation of nutritional calculations and exchange information. Ms. Wheeler offered many valuable suggestions through each step of the book production process. Robyn Webb Associates conducted taste-testing on every recipe and ensured the accuracy and quality of the finished product. Ms. Webb also developed some of the recipes in this book.

The original manuscript was reviewed by Karmeen Kulkarni, MS, RD, CDE, and Madelyn Wheeler, MS, RD, CDE. The final manuscript was reviewed by Sue McLaughlin, RD, CDE. Patty Walsh provided creative illustrations for each title in the series.

Have fun adding variety and zest to your diet with the *Healthy Selects* Series!

American Diabetes Association

PREFACE

Easy & Elegant Entrees is the second cookbook in a new series offering lighter and healthier recipes that still taste wonderful. I served many of these recipes, with great success, at elegant parties and casual dinners. I know you will appreciate the abundance of ways to serve the delicious recipes presented in this series.

My long-term goal was to write and share the results with you. With that in mind, I would like to offer my warmest and most sincere appreciation to the American Diabetes Association in helping me reach my goal. Without their interest and assistance, this series of books would just be another manuscript in my office.

I would like to dedicate this book to my family, who encouraged me to find a wider audience, and to my close friends (who are never without their opinions!) for taste-testing their way through many joyful times.

I hope you enjoy these delicious additions to a varied and healthy diet.

Frank R. Blenn

INTRODUCTION

Packed with tasty and easy-to-prepare recipes for special main dishes, *Easy & Elegant Entrees* is a terrific addition to your cookbook library. Here are some important points to keep in mind as you try the recipes:

♦ The nutrient analysis section *only includes* the ingredients listed in the ingredients section! The nutrient analyses do *not* include serving suggestions sometimes provided in other sections of the recipe. For example, in the recipe for Baked Garlic Scampi, we suggest that it be served over rice. But, because rice is not included as an ingredient, you know that the nutrient analysis only applies to the Baked Garlic Scampi recipe itself. Similarly, garnishes are not included in the analyses (unless they are included in the ingredients list).

♦ In general, we have suggested using olive oil instead of low-calorie margarine. You can use low-calorie margarine if you prefer, depending on your individual nutrition goals. Olive oil provides more monounsaturated fats, but low-calorie margarine contains fewer calories. Feel free to interchange them if you need to.

♦ If you can find a version of an ingredient lower in fat than the items we used, feel free to use it instead. The recipes will still work, and your total fat grams will go down slightly. We usually use low-fat options, defined as containing 3 grams of fat or less per serving. When we use the term low-calorie, that means 40 calories or less per serving.

♦ Remember that when a food is listed as a Free Food, there may still be limits on the serving size. For example, for many dressings and toppings, only 2 Tbsp. or less is free. More than that, and the food has an exchange value. Also, in terms of nutrient values, 1 Starch/Bread Exchange can be interchanged with 1 Fruit Exchange.

♦ Note that the serving sizes are not uniform and vary from recipe to recipe.

Good luck, and we hope you enjoy *Easy & Elegant Entrees!*

SENSATIONAL SEAFOOD

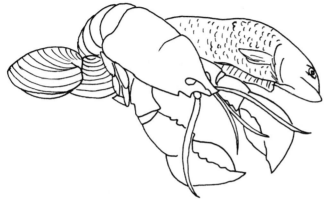

HINTS FOR BUYING AND PREPARING DELICIOUS FISH

◆ When buying whole fish, look for bright, clear eyes; red gills; bright, tight scales; and shiny skins. Stale fish have cloudy, sunken eyes; with age, gill color fades to a light pink. The flesh should be firm and springy. When buying fillets, look for freshly-cut flesh, firm in texture, without a dried or brown look. When buying frozen fillets, the wrapping should be made of moisture-proof material and have little or no odor. Look for solidly frozen flesh with clear color, free of ice crystals. Discoloration, a brownish tinge, or a covering of ice crystals all indicate that the fish may have been thawed and refrozen.

◆ To store fresh fish, keep fish and shellfish loosely wrapped in the refrigerator and cook within one day. To store frozen fish, keep fish in the original wrapper and use immediately after thawing. Never thaw and refreeze fish, since this will cause moisture loss and texture and flavor changes.

◆ The best way to thaw frozen fish is to leave it in its original wrappings and thaw it in the refrigerator or in cold water. Thawing at room temperature can cause sogginess. Drain the fish well after unwrapping it and blot it dry with paper towels.

BAKED GARLIC SCAMPI

4 servings/serving size: 3 oz.

*S*campi *is always delicious served over a bed of rice. Remember to buy one pound of shrimp, total weight (with shells on).*

- ◆ **1 lb. large shrimp, peeled, deveined, with tails left on**
- ◆ **1/3 cup low-calorie margarine**
- ◆ **7 garlic cloves, crushed**
- ◆ **2 Tbsp. chopped parsley**
- ◆ **1 tsp. grated lemon peel**
- ◆ **1 Tbsp. lemon juice**

1. In a 13x9x2-inch baking pan, melt the margarine in a 400-degree oven. Add the salt, garlic and 1 Tbsp. parsley; mix well.
2. Arrange the shrimp in a single layer in the baking pan and bake at 350 degrees for 3 minutes, uncovered. Turn the shrimp and sprinkle with lemon peel, lemon juice, and the remaining 1 Tbsp. parsley. Continue to bake 1 to 2 minutes more until the shrimp are bright pink and tender.
3. Remove shrimp from oven and arrange on a warm serving platter. Spoon garlic mixture over shrimp and serve.

Lean Meat Exchange	3	Total Carbohydrate	2 grams
Calories	166	Dietary Fiber	0 grams
Total Fat	8 grams	Sugars	2 grams
Saturated Fat	2 grams	Protein	20 grams
Calories from fat	76	Sodium	331 milligrams
Cholesterol	180 milligrams		

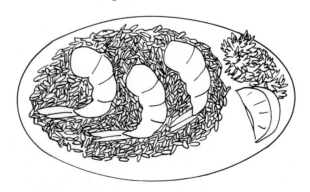

SHRIMP PROVENCAL

8 servings/serving size: 2–3 oz. shrimp with sauce

Serve crusty French bread to soak up this warm shallot and tomato sauce. Remember to buy two pounds of shrimp, total weight (with shells on).

- 2 Tbsp. olive oil
- 1/4 cup chopped shallots
- 1 garlic clove, crushed
- 1 tomato, peeled and coarsely chopped
- 8 oz. tomato sauce
- Dash salt and pepper
- Dash cayenne pepper
- 2 lb. shrimp, shelled, deveined and boiled for 5 minutes (until they just turn pink)
- 1/4 cup dry white wine
- 2 Tbsp. chopped parsley

1. In a large skillet over medium heat, heat the oil. Saute the shallots and garlic for 2 minutes.
2. Add the chopped tomato, tomato sauce, salt, pepper, and cayenne pepper. Bring to a boil, stirring occasionally.
3. Reduce the heat to low and let simmer uncovered for 10 minutes. Stir in the shrimp and wine. Continue to cook for 5 minutes.
4. Remove from the heat and transfer to a serving platter. Sprinkle with parsley and serve.

....

Lean Meat Exchange 2
Calories 117
Total Fat . . . . 4 grams
   Saturated Fat . . . . 1 gram
   Calories from fat 38
Cholesterol . . . . 131 milligrams

Total Carbohydrate . . . . 4 grams
   Dietary Fiber . . . . 1 gram
   Sugars . . . . 2 grams
Protein . . . . 15 grams
Sodium . . . . 354 milligrams

SHRIMP CREOLE*

4 servings/serving size: 2–3 oz. shrimp with 1/2 cup cooked rice

*T*his creole sauce is really versatile—you can add chicken cubes, lobster chunks, mussels or clams instead of shrimp. Remember to buy one pound of shrimp, total weight (with shells on).

- ◆ 8 oz. tomato sauce
- ◆ 1/2 cup sliced mushrooms
- ◆ 1/2 cup dry white wine
- ◆ 1/2 cup chopped onion
- ◆ 2 garlic cloves, minced
- ◆ 1/2 cup chopped celery

- ◆ 2 bay leaves
- ◆ 1/4 tsp. cayenne pepper
- ◆ 1 lb. shrimp, peeled and deveined
- ◆ 2 cups cooked rice, hot

1. In a large skillet, combine the tomato sauce, mushrooms, wine, onion, garlic, green pepper, celery, bay leaves and cayenne pepper. Bring to a boil; cover, reduce the heat and let simmer for 10 to 15 minutes.
2. Add the shrimp to the tomato sauce and cook uncovered for 3 to 5 minutes, until the shrimp are bright pink.
3. To serve, spread the rice on a platter and spoon the shrimp and creole sauce over the rice.

....

Starch/Bread Exchange 2	Cholesterol . . . . 131 milligrams	
Lean Meat Exchange 1	Total Carbohydrate . . . . 31 grams	
Calories 213	Dietary Fiber . . . . 2 grams	
Total Fat . . . . 1 gram	Sugars . . . . 4 grams	
Saturated Fat . . . . 0 grams	Protein . . . . 18 grams	
Calories from fat 10	Sodium . . . . 534 milligrams	

* This recipe is high in sodium! The sodium content can be reduced by using low-sodium tomato sauce.

BAKED SHRIMP AND MUSHROOM CASSEROLE*

8 servings/serving size: 2-1/2–3 oz.

These tender shrimp are covered with a light sherry cream sauce. Remember to buy two pounds of shrimp, total weight (with shells on).

- 6 Tbsp. low-calorie margarine
- 1 lb. mushrooms, sliced
- 2 Tbsp. flour
- 1 tsp. salt
- Fresh ground pepper
- 1/8 tsp. nutmeg
- 1 cup half-and-half
- 1/2 cup dry sherry
- 2 lb. shrimp, peeled, deveined and boiled for 2 minutes
- 1/2 cup unsalted crackers, crushed
- 1 Tbsp. chopped parsley

1. In a large skillet over medium heat, melt 4 Tbsp. of the margarine. Add the mushrooms and saute for 3 to 5 minutes. With a slotted spoon, remove the mushrooms and arrange on the bottom of a 1-1/2-quart baking dish.
2. Whisk flour, salt, pepper and nutmeg in the skillet until smooth. Gradually add the half-and-half and bring to a boil, stirring constantly. Reduce the heat and simmer for 1 to 2 minutes.
3. Add the shrimp and sherry, mixing well. Spoon the shrimp mixture over the mushrooms in the baking dish. Melt the remaining margarine and mix with the cracker crumbs. Sprinkle the cracker crumbs over the shrimp; sprinkle with parsley.
4. Bake uncovered at 350 degrees for 20 minutes until the casserole is heated through and bubbly. Remove from the oven and serve hot.

• •

Medium-Fat Meat Exchange	1	Cholesterol	143 milligrams
Starch/Bread Exchange	1/2	Total Carbohydrate	8 grams
Calories	188	Dietary Fiber	1 gram
Total Fat	9 grams	Sugars	2 grams
Saturated Fat	3 grams	Protein	17 grams
Calories from fat	83	Sodium	534 milligrams

* This recipe is high in sodium!

CRAB MEAT STUFFING

8 servings/serving size: 4 oz.

Use this stuffing to fill the cavity of a zucchini or yellow squash.

- 1/4 cup low-calorie margarine
- 1/4 cup flour
- 1 cup skim milk
- 1/2 Tbsp. Worcestershire sauce
- 2 lb. crab meat, flaked
- 1/4 tsp. nutmeg
- 1 Tbsp. chopped red bell pepper
- 2 Tbsp. minced parsley
- Dash salt
- Fresh ground pepper

1. Melt the margarine in a large skillet over medium heat; add flour and whisk until smooth.
2. Add the milk; continue cooking, stirring constantly, until thickened.
3. Add remaining ingredients; mix thoroughly. Continue to cook until crab meat is heated through.

....

Lean Meat Exchange	2	Cholesterol	97 milligrams
Starch/Bread Exchange	1/2	Total Carbohydrate	5 grams
Calories	150	Dietary Fiber	0 grams
Total Fat	5 grams	Sugars	21 grams
Saturated Fat	1 gram	Protein	21 grams
Calories from fat	41	Sodium	357 milligrams

CRAB IMPERIAL

6 servings/serving size: 3 oz. (1 custard cup)

This dish is suitable to serve as a light party luncheon entree or as an appetizer for dinner.

- ◆ 1 lb. crab meat, flaked
- ◆ 1 egg substitute equivalent, slightly beaten
- ◆ 1/2 cup low-fat mayonnaise
- ◆ 2 Tbsp. skim milk
- ◆ 2 tsp. capers
- ◆ Fresh ground pepper
- ◆ 3 Tbsp. grated Parmesan cheese
- ◆ 1/4 cup chopped parsley

1. Preheat the oven to 350 degrees. In a medium bowl, combine the crab meat, egg, mayonnaise, milk, capers and pepper. Stir until well blended.
2. Coat 6 custard cups with nonstick cooking spray and divide the mixture evenly into the cups. Sprinkle the tops with cheese and bake for 25 to 30 minutes.
3. Remove from the oven and garnish with chopped parsley before serving.

••

Medium-Fat Meat Exchange 2		Total Carbohydrate .... 2 grams	
Calories 143		Dietary Fiber .... 0 grams	
Total Fat .... 8 grams		Sugars .... 1 gram	
Saturated Fat .... 2 grams		Protein .... 15 grams	
Calories from fat 72		Sodium .... 361 milligrams	
Cholesterol .... 75 milligrams			

VEGETABLE SALMON CAKES*

4 servings/serving size: 4 oz.

*C*anned salmon is an excellent source of calcium.

- 1 lb. canned salmon, drained
- 1 cup dry bread crumbs
- 3 medium russet or white potatoes, skinned, cooked and mashed
- 1/2 cup grated carrots
- 1/2 cup minced onion
- 2 Tbsp. fresh lemon juice
- 2 egg substitute equivalents, slightly beaten

1. In a medium bowl, combine the salmon, 1/2 cup of the bread crumbs, potatoes, carrots, onion, lemon juice and eggs, mixing well.
2. Coat a large skillet with nonstick cooking spray and place over medium heat. Form the salmon into patties and coat with remaining bread crumbs.
3. Place the salmon cakes in the heated skillet and cook for 6 minutes per side or until golden brown. Remove from heat, transfer to a serving platter and serve hot.

....

Starch/Bread Exchange	2-1/2	Cholesterol	36 milligrams
Lean Meat Exchange	2	Total Carbohydrate	38 grams
Calories	322	Dietary Fiber	3 grams
Total Fat	7 grams	Sugars	4 grams
Saturated Fat	2 grams	Protein	27 grams
Calories from fat	59	Sodium	729 milligrams

* This recipe is high in sodium! The sodium content can be reduced by making your own bread crumbs (leave some low-sodium bread out on the counter to dry for two days, then crumble). Or see *Great Starts & Fine Finishes* for a Homemade Seasoned Bread Crumbs recipe!

GRILLED SALMON WITH DILL SAUCE

8 servings/serving size: 3–4 oz. salmon with 2 Tbsp. sauce

*P*erk *up plain yogurt with the flavor of dill and moisten these grilled salmon steaks.*

- ♦ **1 cup plain nonfat yogurt**
- ♦ **2 tsp. minced fresh dill**
- ♦ **1/4 cup chopped scallions**
- ♦ **1 tsp. capers**
- ♦ **2 tsp. minced parsley**
- ♦ **1 tsp. minced chives**
- ♦ **1 Tbsp. olive oil**
- ♦ **2 lb. salmon steaks**

1. In a small bowl, combine all the sauce ingredients and set aside. Spray the racks of your grill with nonstick cooking spray.
2. Brush the salmon steaks with olive oil and grill them over medium-hot coals for 4 minutes per side, or just until the salmon flakes with a fork.
3. Transfer the salmon to a platter and serve with dill sauce on the side.

....

Lean Meat Exchange 4
Calories 218
Total Fat . . . . 11 grams
   Saturated Fat . . . . 2 grams
   Calories from fat 103
Cholesterol . . . . 79 milligrams

Total Carbohydrate . . . . 2 grams
   Dietary Fiber . . . . 0 grams
   Sugars . . . . 2 grams
Protein . . . . 26 grams
Sodium . . . . 81 milligrams

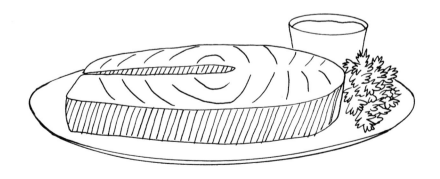

ELEGANT SWORDFISH STEAKS

10 servings/serving size: 3–4 oz.

*T*ry *using tuna, salmon, mahi-mahi or any other thick steaks in this recipe.*

- ◆ **2-1/2 lb. swordfish steaks**
- ◆ **1/2 cup olive oil**
- ◆ **1 cup dry white wine**
- ◆ **1 small onion, minced**

- ◆ **2 tsp. chopped fresh oregano**
- ◆ **2 garlic cloves, minced**
- ◆ **2 Tbsp. fresh lemon juice**
- ◆ **1 large lemon, cut into wedges**

1. Place swordfish steaks in a shallow baking dish. Combine all the ingredients except for the lemon wedges. Pour the mixture over the swordfish steaks and let them marinate 1 hour at room temperature.
2. Spray the grill rack with nonstick cooking spray and cook the swordfish 4 to 5 inches from medium-hot coals for 5 to 6 minutes per side until the fish is opaque (the fish becomes white instead of translucent) throughout. Transfer to a serving platter and garnish with lemon wedges.

....

Lean Meat Exchange 3
Calories 181
Total Fat . . . . 8 grams
    Saturated Fat . . . . 2 grams
    Calories from fat 74
Cholesterol . . . . 48 milligrams

Total Carbohydrate . . . . 0 grams
    Dietary Fiber . . . . 0 grams
    Sugars . . . . 0 grams
Protein . . . . 25 grams
Sodium . . . . 114 milligrams

SAUTEED TROUT ALMANDINE*

4 servings/serving size: 3 oz. with topping

*P*an-dressed trout is gutted, but with the head and tail left on. Ask your fish market to do this for you.

- 1/2 cup flour
- 1/2 tsp. salt (optional)
- Fresh ground pepper
- 4 pan-dressed trout (about 6–8 ounces each)
- 1/3 cup olive oil

- 2 tsp. low-calorie margarine
- 2 Tbsp. fresh lemon juice
- 4 Tbsp. chopped almonds
- 1 lemon, cut into wedges
- Parsley sprigs

1. In a plastic or paper bag combine the flour, salt and pepper. Place the trout one at a time in the bag and shake to coat.
2. Add 3 Tbsp. of the olive oil to a large skillet and saute the trout over medium heat until golden brown on each side (about 4 to 5 minutes per side).
3. Remove the trout from the skillet and transfer to a warm serving platter. Keep warm. Add the remaining oil and margarine to skillet, add the almonds and saute for 2 minutes. Add the lemon juice and cook a few minutes more.
4. Spoon the almonds over the trout and garnish with lemon wedges and parsley.

....

Medium-Fat Meat Exchange 3	Cholesterol . . . . 63 milligrams
Fat Exchange 2-1/2	Total Carbohydrate . . . . 14 grams
Starch/Bread Exchange 1	Dietary Fiber . . . . 1 gram
Calories 425	Sugars . . . . 2 grams
Total Fat . . . . 30 grams	Protein . . . . 26 grams
Saturated Fat . . . . 4 grams	Sodium . . . . 362 milligrams
Calories from fat 266	w/o added salt . . . . . . 75 milligrams

* This recipe is relatively high in fat!

POACHED RED SNAPPER

4 servings/serving size: 4 oz.

*T*he whole fish is presented in this recipe. Have your fish store clean and scale the fish for you, but do leave on the head and tail.

- 1 cup dry white wine
- 1 medium lemon, sliced
- 6 parsley sprigs
- 5 peppercorns
- 5 scallions, sliced
- 2 bay leaves

- 1/2 tsp. salt (optional)
- 1/2 to 1 cup water
- 1-1/2 to 2 lb. dressed red snapper
- 1 lemon, sliced
- Parsley sprigs

1. In a fish poacher or very large skillet, combine the wine, lemon slices, parsley sprigs, peppercorns, scallions, bay leaves, salt and water. Bring the mixture to a boil; add the snapper.
2. Cover the pan, lower the heat and simmer the red snapper for 15 to 20 minutes until the fish flakes easily with a fork.
3. Carefully lift out the snapper and transfer to a platter. Garnish with lemon slices and parsley.

....

Lean Meat Exchange 2	Total Carbohydrate . . . . 0 grams
Calories 111	Dietary Fiber . . . . 0 grams
Total Fat . . . . 2 grams	Sugars . . . . 0 grams
Saturated Fat . . . . 0 grams	Protein . . . . 23 grams
Calories from fat 14	Sodium . . . . 112 milligrams
Cholesterol . . . . 39 milligrams	w/o added salt . . . . . . 48 milligrams

BROILED SOLE WITH MUSTARD SAUCE

6 servings/serving size: 3 oz. with sauce

*T*his delicious sauce keeps fish moist. Try it over cooked broccoli or string beans, too.

- ◆ 1-1/2 lb. fresh sole fillets
- ◆ 3 Tbsp. low-fat mayonnaise
- ◆ 2 Tbsp. Dijon mustard
- ◆ 1 Tbsp. chopped parsley
- ◆ Fresh ground pepper
- ◆ 1 large lemon, cut into wedges

1. Coat a baking sheet with nonstick cooking spray. Arrange fillets so they don't overlap each other.
2. In a small bowl, combine the mayonnaise, mustard, parsley and pepper and mix thoroughly. Spread the mixture evenly over the fillets. Broil 3 to 4 inches from the heat for 4 minutes until fish flakes easily with a fork.
3. Arrange fillets on a serving platter, garnish with lemon wedges and serve.

Lean Meat Exchange 2
Calories 129
Total Fat . . . . 4 grams
  Saturated Fat . . . . 1 gram
  Calories from fat 34
Cholesterol . . . . 63 milligrams
Total Carbohydrate . . . . 1 gram
  Dietary Fiber . . . . 0 grams
  Sugars . . . . 1 gram
Protein . . . . 22 grams
Sodium . . . . 201 milligrams

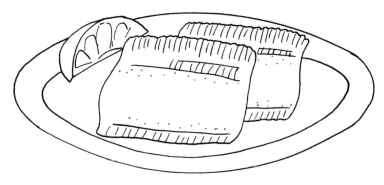

LOBSTER FRICASSEE

4 servings/serving size: 1/2 cup fricassee with 1/2 cup pasta or rice

A fricassee is traditionally served in a white sauce, but this low-fat version tastes just as good!

- **2 cups shelled lobster meat**
- **1/4 cup low-fat margarine**
- **3/4 lb. mushrooms, sliced**
- **1/2 tsp. onion powder**
- **1/2 cup skim milk**
- **1/4 cup flour**
- **1/4 tsp. paprika**
- **Dash salt and pepper**
- **2 cups cooked rice or pasta**
- **Parsley sprigs**

1. Cut the lobster meat into bite-size pieces. Melt the margarine in a saucepan; add the mushrooms and onion powder. Saute for 5 to 6 minutes.
2. Whisk the milk and flour in a small bowl, whisking quickly to eliminate any lumps. Pour milk mixture into mushroom mixture; mix thoroughly, and continue cooking for 3 to 5 minutes.
3. Add the lobster, paprika, salt and pepper; continue cooking for 5 to 10 minutes until lobster is heated through.
4. Spread rice or pasta onto a serving platter, spoon lobster and sauce over the top and garnish with parsley to serve.

....

Starch/Bread Exchange 2	Cholesterol .... 39 milligrams
Medium-Fat Meat Exchange 1	Total Carbohydrate .... 29 grams
Calories 244	Dietary Fiber .... 4 grams
Total Fat .... 6 grams	Sugars .... 4 grams
Saturated Fat .... 1 gram	Protein .... 17 grams
Calories from fat 58	Sodium .... 349 milligrams

SEA BASS WITH GINGER SAUCE*

2 servings/serving size: 3–4 oz.

Steaming fish is the healthiest way to prepare it—and it's always moist, never dried out.

- ♦ 2 sea bass fillets, 4 oz. each
- ♦ 2 Tbsp. peanut oil
- ♦ 2 Tbsp. minced fresh ginger
- ♦ 2 garlic cloves, minced
- ♦ 1/3 cup minced scallions
- ♦ 4 tsp. chopped cilantro
- ♦ 2 Tbsp. lite soy sauce

1. In a medium steamer, add water and bring to a boil. Arrange the fillets on the steamer rack. Cover and steam for 6 to 8 minutes.
2. Meanwhile, heat the oil in a small skillet. Add the ginger and garlic and saute for 2 to 3 minutes.
3. Transfer the steamed fillets to a platter. Pour ginger oil over the fillets and top with scallions, cilantro and soy sauce.

....

Medium-Fat Meat Exchange	3	Cholesterol	45 milligrams
Vegetable Exchange	1	Total Carbohydrate	3 grams
Calories	244	Dietary Fiber	0 grams
Total Fat	16 grams	Sugars	3 grams
Saturated Fat	3 grams	Protein	21 grams
Calories from fat	145	Sodium	676 milligrams

* This recipe is high in sodium due to the soy sauce. If you need to cut down on sodium, simply omit that ingredient.

FRESH FLOUNDER CREOLE

4 servings/serving size: 3 oz. fish with creole sauce and garnish

Add a touch of New Orleans to dinner!

- 1 lb. flounder fillets
- 3/4 cup chopped tomato
- 1/4 cup chopped green pepper
- 3 Tbsp. fresh lemon juice
- 1-1/2 tsp. olive oil
- 2 tsp. hot pepper sauce (Tabasco)

- 1 tsp. finely chopped onion
- 1/2 tsp. dried basil
- 1/2 tsp. celery seed
- 1 large green pepper, sliced into rings
- 1 tomato, cut into wedges

1. Preheat the oven to 400 degrees. Spray a 13x9x2-inch baking dish with nonstick cooking spray; place fillets in the dish. In a medium bowl combine all the ingredients except for the garnish; mix thoroughly.
2. Spoon creole mixture over fillets and bake for 10 minutes or until fish flakes easily with a fork. Transfer to a platter and garnish with pepper rings and tomato wedges to serve.

Lean Meat Exchange	2	Cholesterol	59 milligrams
Vegetable Exchange	2	Total Carbohydrate	9 grams
Calories	155	Dietary Fiber	2 grams
Total Fat	3 grams	Sugars	6 grams
Saturated Fat	1 gram	Protein	23 grams
Calories from fat	30	Sodium	102 milligrams

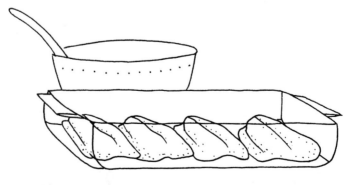

PAN-FRIED SCALLOPS

6 servings/serving size: 3–4 oz. with 1/3 cup rice

Some people think scallops taste best when they are lightly pan-fried, which seals in all the natural juices.

- 1/2 cup fine dried bread crumbs
- 1/4 tsp. paprika
- Dash salt and pepper
- 1-1/2 lb. scallops
- 1/4 cup olive oil
- 1 Tbsp. low-calorie margarine
- 1/4 cup dry white wine
- 2 cups cooked rice, hot

1. Combine the bread crumbs, paprika, salt and pepper in a small bowl. Roll the scallops thoroughly in the bread crumb mixture.
2. In a large skillet, heat the olive oil and margarine and saute the scallops quickly for about 2 to 3 minutes until lightly browned.
3. Spread the hot cooked rice on a serving platter and gently place the cooked scallops on top of the rice. Add the white wine to the remaining olive oil/margarine mixture in the pan. Bring to a slow boil. Remove from heat and pour over the rice and scallops to serve.

....

Medium-Fat Meat Exchange	2	Cholesterol	39 milligrams
Starch/Bread Exchange	1-1/2	Total Carbohydrate	22 grams
Calories	280	Dietary Fiber	1 gram
Total Fat	12 grams	Sugars	1 gram
Saturated Fat	2 grams	Protein	20 grams
Calories from fat	104	Sodium	312 milligrams

GRILLED SCALLOP KABOBS

6 servings/serving size: 1 kabob

Your guests will have fun preparing their own kabobs. If you're using wooden skewers, be sure to soak them in hot water for 15 minutes before you thread on the food. This will prevent the ends of the skewers from burning on the grill.

- **15 oz. pineapple chunks, packed in their own juice, undrained**
- **1/4 cup dry white wine**
- **1/4 cup lite soy sauce**
- **2 Tbsp. minced parsley**
- **Fresh ground pepper**
- **1 lb. scallops**
- **18 large cherry tomatoes**
- **1 large green pepper, cut into 1-inch squares**
- **18 medium mushroom caps**

1. Drain the pineapple, reserving the juice. In a shallow baking dish, combine the pineapple juice, wine, soy sauce, parsley, garlic and pepper. Mix well.
2. Add the pineapple, scallops, tomatoes, peppers, and mushrooms. Marinate 30 minutes at room temperature, stirring occasionally.
3. Alternate pineapple, scallops and vegetables on skewers. Grill the kabobs over medium hot coals about 4 to 5 inches from the heat, basting and turning frequently, for 5 to 7 minutes.

....

Vegetable Exchange 2	Cholesterol . . . . 26 milligrams
Lean Meat Exchange 1	Total Carbohydrate . . . . 13 grams
Calories 112	Dietary Fiber . . . . 3 grams
Total Fat . . . . 1 gram	Sugars . . . . 8 grams
Saturated Fat . . . . 0 grams	Protein . . . . 13 grams
Calories from fat 11	Sodium . . . . 240 milligrams

MARVELOUS MEATS

STEAK WITH BRANDIED ONIONS

4 servings/serving size: 2–3 oz. steak with onions

- ◆ **12 oz. lean sirloin steak**
- ◆ **4 Tbsp. low-calorie margarine**
- ◆ **1/2 tsp. garlic powder**
- ◆ **4 medium onions, sliced**
- ◆ **1 Tbsp. chopped fresh parsley**
- ◆ **Dash brandy**

Prepare the sirloin steak to your liking. In a medium skillet, melt the margarine and garlic. Add the onions and parsley, sauteing until onions are tender. Add brandy and let simmer for 1 to 2 minutes. Transfer steak to platter, spoon brandied onions over the top and serve.

Lean Meat Exchange 3	Cholesterol . . . . 56 milligrams
Vegetable Exchange 2	Total Carbohydrate . . . . 11 grams
Fat Exchange 1/2	Dietary Fiber . . . . 2 grams
Calories 230	Sugars . . . . 7 grams
Total Fat . . . . 11 grams	Protein . . . . 21 grams
Saturated Fat . . . . 3 grams	Sodium . . . . 137 milligrams
Calories from fat 102	

BRANDIED STEAKS WITH MUSTARD SAUCE

4 servings/serving size: one 5–6 oz. steak

You'll want to save this filet mignon dish for special occasions, since it is relatively high in fat and calories!

- ◆ 6 Tbsp. low-calorie margarine
- ◆ Fresh ground pepper
- ◆ 4 filet mignon steaks, 5–6 oz. each
- ◆ 4 large shallots, sliced
- ◆ 6 Tbsp. brandy
- ◆ 2 cups low-sodium beef broth
- ◆ 2 Tbsp. vegetable oil
- ◆ Chives, minced

1. In a large skillet, melt 1 Tbsp. of the margarine over medium heat. Season the steaks with pepper. Add the steaks to the skillet and cook for 2 to 3 minutes per side. Transfer steaks to a heated platter and keep warm.
2. Melt 1 Tbsp. of the margarine in the skillet, add the sliced shallots and saute for 1 to 2 minutes. Remove from heat and let cool for 1 to 2 minutes. Add brandy and ignite with a long match. When flames subside, add broth and bring to a boil over high heat. Boil 8 to 10 minutes or until syrupy.
3. Whisk in oil, mustard and remaining 4 Tbsp. margarine. Season with pepper and spoon sauce over steaks. Garnish with chives to serve.

• •

Medium-Fat Meat Exchange 5	Cholesterol .... 100 milligrams
Fat Exchange 1-1/2	Total Carbohydrate .... 3 grams
Calories 447	Dietary Fiber .... 0 grams
Total Fat .... 32 grams	Sugars .... 2 grams
Saturated Fat .... 9 grams	Protein .... 33 grams
Calories from fat 288	Sodium .... 239 milligrams

BAKED STEAK WITH CREOLE SAUCE

4 servings/serving size: 3–4 oz.

This spicy creole sauce helps to keep the steak tender and juicy.

- 2 tsp. olive oil
- 1/4 cup chopped onion
- 1/4 cup chopped green pepper
- 8 oz. canned tomatoes
- 1/2 tsp. chili powder
- 1/4 tsp. celery seed
- 1/2 tsp. garlic powder
- 1 lb. lean boneless round steak

1. In a large skillet over medium heat, heat the oil. Add the onions and green pepper and saute until onions are translucent (about 5 minutes).
2. Add the tomatoes and the seasonings; cover and let simmer over low heat for 20 to 25 minutes. This allows the flavors to blend.
3. Trim all visible fat off the steak. In a nonstick pan or a pan that has been sprayed with nonstick cooking spray, lightly brown the steak on each side. Transfer the steak to a 13x9x2-inch baking dish; pour the sauce over the steak and cover.
4. Bake at 350 degrees for 1-1/4 hours or until steak is tender. Remove from oven; slice steak and arrange on a serving platter. Spoon sauce over the steak and serve.

....

Lean Meat Exchange 3	Cholesterol . . . . 66 milligrams
Vegetable Exchange 1	Total Carbohydrate . . . . 4 grams
Calories 195	Dietary Fiber . . . . 1 gram
Total Fat . . . . 9 grams	Sugars . . . . 2 grams
Saturated Fat . . . . 3 grams	Protein . . . . 24 grams
Calories from fat 81	Sodium . . . . 150 milligrams

BEEF PROVENCAL

4 servings/serving size: 4 oz.

*F*resh zucchini and cherry tomatoes add color to this easy-to-make dish.

- 3 garlic cloves, minced
- 1 tsp. dried basil
- Fresh ground pepper
- 2 tsp. olive oil
- 4 lean beef cube steaks, 4 oz. each

- 2 small zucchini, thinly sliced
- 6 cherry tomatoes, halved
- 3/4 cup grated Parmesan cheese

1. In a small bowl combine the garlic, basil and pepper. Divide the mixture in half and rub one half of this mixture on both sides of the steaks. Reserve remaining seasonings.
2. In a large skillet over medium heat, heat the oil. Add the seasonings and heat for 30 seconds. Add the zucchini and saute for 3 minutes. Add the tomatoes and continue sauteing for 1 to 2 minutes. Remove from heat and transfer to a serving platter, sprinkle with cheese and keep warm.
3. Add the steaks, 2 at a time, and pan-fry until desired degree of doneness; transfer to a platter. Spoon remaining juices over the steaks and serve them with the vegetables.

....

Lean Meat Exchange 4	Cholesterol . . . . 91 milligrams
Vegetable Exchange 1	Total Carbohydrate . . . . 5 grams
Fat Exchange 1/2	Dietary Fiber . . . . 1 gram
Calories 275	Sugars . . . . 3 grams
Total Fat . . . . 13 grams	Protein . . . . 33 grams
Saturated Fat . . . . 5 grams	Sodium . . . . 328 milligrams
Calories from fat 120	

BUTTERFLIED BEEF EYE ROAST

12 servings/serving size: 3–4 oz.

*S*ince this is a large piece of meat, be sure to let it marinate overnight or even for two days.

- ◆ **3-lb. lean beef eye roast, butterflied**
- ◆ **3 Tbsp. olive oil**
- ◆ **1/4 cup water**
- ◆ **1/2 cup red wine vinegar**
- ◆ **3 garlic cloves, minced**
- ◆ **1/2 tsp. crushed red pepper**
- ◆ **1 Tbsp. chopped fresh thyme**

1. Slice the roast down the middle, open it and lay it flat in a shallow baking dish. In a small bowl combine the remaining ingredients and pour the mixture over the roast. Cover and let the meat marinate at least 12 hours. Turn the roast occasionally.
2. Remove the roast from the marinade and place on a rack in the broiler pan. Broil the roast 5 to 7 inches from the heat, turning and basting occasionally, for 20 to 25 minutes or until desired degree of doneness.
3. Remove from oven, cover with foil and let stand for 15 to 20 minutes before carving. Transfer to a serving platter, spoon remaining juices over the top and serve.

· ·

Lean Meat Exchange 3	Total Carbohydrate . . . . 1 gram
Calories 168	Dietary Fiber . . . . 0 grams
Total Fat . . . . 7 grams	Sugars . . . . 1 gram
Saturated Fat . . . . 2 grams	Protein . . . . 24 grams
Calories from fat 64	Sodium . . . . 51 milligrams
Cholesterol . . . . 57 milligrams	

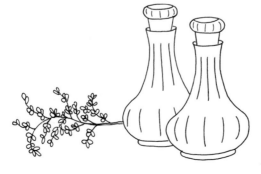

MARINATED BEEF KABOBS

6 servings/serving size: 1 kabob

The marinade for this dish is quite tasty and easy to prepare. Try it with chicken, too.

- 1-1/2 lb. lean sirloin steak, cut into 1-1/2-inch cubes
- 1 large red onion, cut into 1-inch cubes
- 1 each large green and red bell peppers, cut into 1-inch squares
- 1/2 lb. mushrooms, stems removed
- 1/2 cup low-calorie Italian salad dressing
- 1/4 cup burgundy wine

1. Place cubed meat and prepared vegetables together in a shallow dish. In a small bowl, combine the salad dressing and wine; blend well. Pour the marinade over the meat and vegetables. Cover, refrigerate and let marinate for at least 8 hours, stirring occasionally.
2. Alternate the meat and vegetables on 6 skewers. Grill kabobs over medium heat, basting and turning often, for 15 to 20 minutes or until desired degree of doneness. Arrange on a platter and serve.

....

Lean Meat Exchange 3
Vegetable Exchange 2
Calories 232
Total Fat . . . . 8 grams
   Saturated Fat . . . . 3 grams
   Calories from fat 75
Cholesterol . . . . 74 milligrams
Total Carbohydrate . . . . 11 grams
   Dietary Fiber . . . . 2 grams
   Sugars . . . . 5 grams
Protein . . . . 28 grams
Sodium . . . . 344 milligrams

STEAK DIANE*

2 servings/serving size: one 5–6 oz. steak

*T*his classic recipe makes any occasion special.

- **2 beef tenderloin fillets, 5–6 oz. each**
- **1 Tbsp. flour**
- **Dash salt (optional)**
- **Fresh ground pepper**
- **1/4 cup low-calorie margarine**
- **1 tsp. Dijon mustard**
- **6 large mushrooms, sliced**
- **2 medium scallions, sliced**
- **2 tsp. Worcestershire sauce**
- **1/4 cup cognac**
- **1/2 cup low-sodium beef broth**
- **2 Tbsp. chopped parsley**

1. Pound steak with a meat mallet, then coat with a mixture of flour, salt and pepper. In a large skillet, melt 1 Tbsp. of the margarine over medium heat.
2. Brown meat quickly, about 1 minute on each side; transfer meat to a platter. Spread meat on both sides with mustard; set aside.
3. Melt remaining margarine in the skillet and saute the mushrooms and onions over medium heat. Add the cognac and ignite with a long match. Let the flames subside, then add beef broth.
4. Return the steaks to the skillet; cook until desired doneness, turning only once. Remove from heat, transfer to a platter, garnish with parsley and serve.

· ·

Medium-Fat Meat Exchange	5	Cholesterol	91 milligrams
Starch/Bread Exchange	1/2	Total Carbohydrate	9 grams
Calories	415	Dietary Fiber	1 gram
Total Fat	26 grams	Sugars	3 grams
Saturated Fat	8 grams	Protein	32 grams
Calories from fat	234	Sodium	346 milligrams

* This recipe is relatively high in fat!

STUFFED BELL PEPPERS*

4 servings/serving size: 1 pepper with sauce

*T*ry using this basic filling to stuff zucchini or yellow squash, too.

- ◆ 4 medium peppers, red or green (or both)
- ◆ 1 lb. lean ground sirloin
- ◆ 1 small onion, chopped
- ◆ 1/3 cup instant white rice
- ◆ 1 tsp. dried oregano
- ◆ Fresh ground pepper
- ◆ 8 oz. canned tomato sauce
- ◆ 1/4 cup burgundy wine
- ◆ Grated Parmesan cheese to taste

1. Slice off the stem end of each pepper and remove the seeds. In a medium bowl, combine the beef, onion, rice, oregano, salt, pepper and 1/3 cup tomato sauce; mix well.
2. Stuff the mixture into the peppers and place them in a medium saucepan. Pour the wine and remaining tomato sauce over peppers.
3. Bring the peppers to a boil; cover and let simmer until they are tender, about 45 minutes. Add a few tablespoons of water if the sauce begins to cook away. Transfer to a serving platter, top with Parmesan cheese and serve.

••

Lean Meat Exchange	3	Cholesterol	71 milligrams
Vegetable Exchange	2	Total Carbohydrate	21 grams
Starch/Bread Exchange	1/2	Dietary Fiber	2 grams
Calories	251	Sugars	6 grams
Total Fat	6 grams	Protein	28 grams
Saturated Fat	2 grams	Sodium	469 milligrams
Calories from fat	54		

* This recipe is high in sodium due to the use of canned tomato sauce! The sodium content can be reduced by using low-sodium tomato sauce.

VEAL PICCATA WITH ORANGE SAUCE

4 servings/serving size: 3–4 oz.

Fresh orange juice and sage make all the difference in this recipe—but they do need to be fresh!

- ◆ **1 lb. lean veal cutlets**
- ◆ **1/2 cup flour**
- ◆ **Dash salt and pepper**
- ◆ **6 Tbsp. low-calorie margarine**

- ◆ **1 cup fresh orange juice**
- ◆ **1 tsp. minced fresh sage**
- ◆ **1 orange, sliced**
- ◆ **1 Tbsp. minced fresh parsley**

1. Place flour on a large plate and season with pepper and salt. In a large skillet, melt 4 Tbsp. of margarine. Coat the veal with flour, shaking off excess. Add to the skillet, in batches, and cook for 30 seconds on each side. Transfer to a warm plate and keep warm.

2. Discard the pan drippings. Add 1/2 cup of the orange juice to the pan and bring to a boil, scraping up any browned bits. Boil for 1 to 2 minutes or until juice is reduced to a glaze.

3. Add remaining 1/2 cup orange juice and sage; season with salt and pepper and bring back to a boil. Boil for 1 to 2 minutes or until mixture thickens.

4. Remove from heat and whisk in remaining 2 Tbsp. of margarine. Transfer veal to a platter, spoon orange sauce on top and garnish with orange slices and fresh parsley to serve.

••

Lean Meat Exchange	4	Cholesterol	117 milligrams
Starch/Bread Exchange	1	Total Carbohydrate	18 grams
Calories	320	Dietary Fiber	1 gram
Total Fat	12 grams	Sugars	8 grams
Saturated Fat	3 grams	Protein	34 grams
Calories from fat	106	Sodium	204 milligrams

VEAL SCALLOPINI

4 servings/serving size: 3–4 oz.

Serve this great dish with vermicelli and steamed broccoli or green beans.

- 4 lean veal cutlets (3–4 ounces each)
- Fresh ground pepper
- 1 Tbsp. olive oil
- 1/2 lb. fresh mushrooms, sliced
- 1 large green pepper, cut into 1/2-inch strips
- 1/2 cup dry white wine
- 1/3 cup low-sodium chicken broth
- 1 Tbsp. lemon juice
- 1 Tbsp. cornstarch
- 2 Tbsp. water
- 2 Tbsp. minced fresh parsley

1. Place the veal cutlets between two pieces of waxed paper and pound until the cutlets are 1/8 inch thick. Sprinkle the veal with pepper and set aside.
2. Over medium heat, heat the oil in a large skillet. Add the veal, a few pieces at a time, cooking 2 to 3 minutes per side or until lightly browned. Remove from skillet and keep the veal warm while you prepare the sauce.
3. Saute the mushrooms and green pepper in the skillet for 3 minutes. Add the wine, broth and lemon juice and bring to a boil. Dissolve the cornstarch with the water and add to the skillet, stirring constantly until mixture has thickened.
4. Remove from heat and stir in the parsley. Arrange the veal on a serving platter and pour the sauce over the top.

....

Lean Meat Exchange	4	Cholesterol	117 milligrams
Vegetable Exchange	1	Total Carbohydrate	7 grams
Calories	252	Dietary Fiber	1 gram
Total Fat	8 grams	Sugars	2 grams
Saturated Fat	2 grams	Protein	34 grams
Calories from fat	76	Sodium	68 milligrams

VEAL ROMANO

6 servings/serving size: 3–4 oz.

You can buy the roasted peppers for this dish in the condiment aisle of the supermarket (they come in jars) or in a gourmet deli.

- 2 Tbsp. olive oil
- 1-1/2 lb. lean veal cutlets
- 1/4 cup flour
- Fresh ground pepper
- 2 Tbsp. low-calorie margarine
- 1/2 cup dry white wine

- 1/2 cup roasted red peppers, drained and julienned
- 8 large black olives, thinly sliced
- 2 Tbsp. capers, rinsed and drained

1. Heat the oil in a skillet over high heat. Place the cutlets between two pieces of waxed paper and pound with a meat mallet until they are about 1/4 inch thick.
2. Lightly flour the veal, shaking off the excess, and add to the skillet. Saute the veal for 2 to 3 minutes on each side, transfer to a platter and sprinkle with pepper. Continue until all veal is cooked.
3. Melt the margarine in the skillet over high heat. Add the wine and scrape the brown bits from the skillet. Reduce heat to medium and add the peppers, olives and capers, stirring occasionally.
4. Continue cooking until heated through. Spoon the sauce over the veal and serve.

....

Lean Meat Exchange 4	Cholesterol . . . . 117 milligrams
Starch/Bread Exchange 1/2	Total Carbohydrate . . . . 5 grams
Calories 270	Dietary Fiber . . . . 1 gram
Total Fat . . . . 12 grams	Sugars . . . . 1 gram
Saturated Fat . . . . 3 grams	Protein . . . . 33 grams
Calories from fat 106	Sodium . . . . 189 milligrams

PORK CHOPS NICOISE

6 servings/serving size: 1 pork chop with topping and 1/3 cup cooked rice

This one-skillet dish is easy to make, but elegant to serve!

- ◆ 1 Tbsp. olive oil
- ◆ 6 lean pork chops (3–4 ounces each)
- ◆ 4 large tomatoes, chopped
- ◆ 2 garlic cloves, minced
- ◆ 1 large green pepper, chopped
- ◆ 1 tsp. dried basil
- ◆ 1/2 cup whole black olives
- ◆ 2 cups cooked rice, hot

1. In a large skillet, heat oil over medium heat. Add pork chops and lightly brown on both sides.
2. Add the tomatoes, garlic, pepper and basil; cover. Simmer for 25 to 30 minutes, turning pork chops once. Add the olives and continue to simmer over low heat for 7 to 10 minutes.
3. Arrange rice on serving platter, place pork chops over rice, spoon sauce over the top and serve.

....

Medium-Fat Meat Exchange	2	Cholesterol	51 milligrams
Starch/Bread Exchange	1-1/2	Total Carbohydrate	25 grams
Calories	275	Dietary Fiber	3 grams
Total Fat	12 grams	Sugars	6 grams
Saturated Fat	3 grams	Protein	18 grams
Calories from fat	105	Sodium	155 milligrams

ITALIAN PORK CHOPS*

4 servings/serving size: 1 pork chop with sauce

Serve this with fresh steamed broccoli and either flavored rice or shaped pasta.

- **4 lean pork chops (about 3–4 ounces each)**
- **Fresh ground pepper**
- **1/2 lb. fresh mushrooms, sliced**
- **1 medium onion, chopped**
- **2 garlic cloves, crushed**
- **2 medium green peppers, julienned**
- **16 oz. canned tomato sauce**
- **1/4 cup dry sherry**
- **1 Tbsp. fresh lemon juice**
- **1/4 tsp. dried oregano**
- **1/4 tsp. dried basil**

1. Trim all excess fat from the pork chops and sprinkle with pepper. Coat a large skillet with nonstick cooking spray, place chops in skillet and brown on both sides.
2. Drain pork chops on paper towels and transfer to a 2-quart baking dish. Cover the chops with the mushrooms and set aside.
3. Saute the onions, garlic and green peppers over medium heat until the onions are tender. Stir in the tomato sauce, sherry, lemon juice, oregano and basil; let simmer, uncovered, for 10 to 15 minutes.
4. Pour tomato mixture over pork chops; cover and let bake at 350 degrees for 40 minutes or until pork chops are tender. Remove from oven and serve.

....

Lean Meat Exchange 3	Cholesterol . . . . 77 milligrams
Starch/Bread Exchange 1	Total Carbohydrate . . . . 20 grams
Vegetable Exchange 1	Dietary Fiber . . . . 3 grams
Calories 295	Sugars . . . . 8 grams
Total Fat . . . . 13 grams	Protein . . . . 27 grams
Saturated Fat . . . . 4 grams	Sodium . . . . 803 milligrams
Calories from fat 113	

* This dish is high in sodium due to the use of canned tomato sauce! The sodium content can be reduced by using low-sodium tomato sauce.

LAMB CHOPS WITH ORANGE SAUCE

Makes 4 servings/serving size: 2 lamb chops with sauce

*T*ry *serving these delicious orange-scented lamb chops with baby peas or french green beans.*

- ◆ 1/2 cup unsweetened orange juice
- ◆ 1 Tbsp. orange rind
- ◆ 1/2 tsp. dried thyme
- ◆ Fresh ground pepper

- ◆ 8 lean lamb chops, about 1/2 inch thick
- ◆ 1 Tbsp. low-calorie margarine
- ◆ 1 cup sliced fresh mushrooms
- ◆ 1/2 cup dry white wine

1. In a shallow baking dish, combine the orange juice, orange rind, thyme and pepper; mix well. Trim all excess fat from lamb chops and place in a baking dish. Spoon orange juice mixture over chops; cover and refrigerate for 3 to 4 hours, occasionally turning chops.

2. Coat a large skillet with nonstick cooking spray; place over medium-high heat until hot. Remove the chops from the marinade, reserving marinade; arrange in the skillet. Brown chops on both sides, remove from skillet and drain.

3. Reduce heat to medium and melt margarine. Add mushrooms and saute until just tender. Stir in reserved marinade and wine and bring to a boil.

4. Return lamb chops to skillet; cover, reduce heat and simmer for 10 to 12 minutes or until sauce is reduced to about 1/2 cup. Transfer lamb chops to platter, spoon orange sauce on top and serve.

....

Lean Meat Exchange	3	Cholesterol	72 milligrams
Starch/Bread Exchange	1/2	Total Carbohydrate	5 grams
Calories	210	Dietary Fiber	1 gram
Total Fat	10 grams	Sugars	4 grams
Saturated Fat	3 grams	Protein	23 grams
Calories from fat	86	Sodium	88 milligrams

LAMB KABOBS

6 servings/serving size: 1 kabob

These fresh, colorful kabobs are especially good served with wild rice.

- 1/2 cup low-calorie Italian salad dressing
- 1/4 cup fresh lemon juice
- 1 tsp. dried oregano
- Fresh ground pepper
- 1-1/2 lb. lean boneless lamb, cut into 2-inch pieces

- 1/2 lb. mushrooms, stems removed
- 10 cherry tomatoes
- 1 red pepper, cut into 1-inch squares
- 1/2 yellow squash, cut into 1-inch chunks

1. In a shallow baking dish, combine the salad dressing, lemon juice, oregano and pepper; mix thoroughly. Add lamb; cover, refrigerate and let marinate for 6 hours or overnight.
2. Remove meat from marinade. Thread the lamb, alternating with vegetables, onto 6 skewers. Broil the skewers 7 to 8 inches from the heat for 18 to 20 minutes, basting frequently with the marinade. Transfer to a platter and serve.

Lean Meat Exchange	3	Cholesterol	76 milligrams
Vegetable Exchange	1	Total Carbohydrate	6 grams
Calories	210	Dietary Fiber	2 grams
Total Fat	9 grams	Sugars	4 grams
Saturated Fat	3 grams	Protein	25 grams
Calories from fat	84	Sodium	356 milligrams

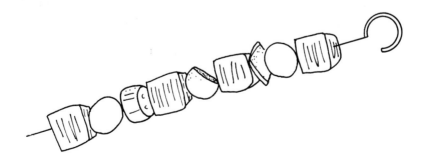

MARINATED LEG OF LAMB

16 servings/serving size: 3-1/2–4 oz.

*M*arinating one to two days is the secret to a great leg of lamb. Serve
with steamed carrots and oven-roasted potatoes.

- ◆ **7-lb. leg of lamb, boned and butterflied**
- ◆ **3 cups dry red wine**
- ◆ **1/4 cup olive oil**
- ◆ **2 medium onions, sliced**
- ◆ **1 large carrot, thinly sliced**
- ◆ **6 parsley stems**

- ◆ **2 bay leaves, crumbled**
- ◆ **2 medium cloves garlic, minced**
- ◆ **Dash salt (optional)**
- ◆ **Fresh ground pepper**
- ◆ **Fresh parsley sprigs**

1. In a large ceramic, glass or stainless steel dish (anything but plastic), combine all the ingredients; cover, refrigerate, and let marinate for 1 to 2 days, turning occasionally.
2. After marinating, drain lamb and pat dry. Place lamb into a grill basket. Broil the lamb 3 to 4 inches from the heat for 15 to 20 minutes per side.
3. Transfer lamb to a cutting board and let cool slightly. Carve lamb diagonally; transfer to serving platter, garnish with parsley sprigs and serve.

....

Lean Meat Exchange	4	Total Carbohydrate	0 grams
Calories	203	Dietary Fiber	0 grams
Total Fat	9 grams	Sugars	0 grams
Saturated Fat	3 grams	Protein	27 grams
Calories from fat	85	Sodium	76 milligrams
Cholesterol	86 milligrams	w/o added salt	67 milligrams

LAMB CURRY

6 servings/serving size: 1/6 curry with 1/3 cup cooked rice

*Y*our guests will appreciate this exotic curry—warm and satisfying on a cold winter night!

- 2 Tbsp. low-calorie margarine
- 2 cups chopped onion
- 1 garlic clove, minced
- 1-1/2 lb. boneless, lean lamb, cut into 1-inch cubes
- 3 Tbsp. flour
- Dash salt
- 1 Tbsp. curry powder
- 1/4 tsp. nutmeg
- 1-1/2 cups low-sodium chicken broth
- 16 oz. low-sodium canned tomatoes, chopped
- 1 large tart apple, pared and cubed
- 2 cups cooked rice, hot

1. In a large skillet over medium heat, melt margarine. Add onion, garlic and lamb; cook together until lamb is browned. Remove lamb and onion from the skillet with a slotted spoon; set aside.
2. In a small bowl, combine the flour, salt, curry powder and nutmeg. Add to the skillet and blend well. Add the chicken broth, stirring constantly until smooth and bubbly.
3. Add chopped tomatoes and liquid, lamb, onion, and apple; blend well. Cover and let simmer over low heat, stirring occasionally, for 45 minutes or until meat is tender. Remove from heat.
4. Spread rice over a serving platter, arrange lamb curry over rice and serve.

....

Lean Meat Exchange	3	Cholesterol	76 milligrams
Starch/Bread Exchange	2	Total Carbohydrate	34 grams
Vegetable Exchange	1	Dietary Fiber	2 grams
Calories	349	Sugars	14 grams
Total Fat	11 grams	Protein	27 grams
Saturated Fat	4 grams	Sodium	150 milligrams
Calories from fat	99		

CREATIVE CHICKEN

MARINATED CHICKEN KABOBS

4 servings/serving size: 3–4 oz.

- ♦ 4 tsp. fresh lemon juice
- ♦ 1/2 tsp. cayenne pepper
- ♦ Fresh ground pepper
- ♦ 1-inch piece of fresh ginger, peeled and minced
- ♦ 1 tsp. curry powder
- ♦ 4 tsp. olive oil
- ♦ 2 whole boneless, skinless chicken breasts, halved, cut into 1/4-inch strips

In a medium bowl, combine all ingredients except the chicken. Add the chicken and let marinate overnight in the refrigerator. Thread the chicken onto metal or wooden skewers. Grill over medium heat until chicken is cooked throughout, about 15 minutes. Transfer to a platter and serve.

Lean Meat Exchange 3
Calories 181
Total Fat . . . . 7 grams
   Saturated Fat . . . . 1 gram
   Calories from fat 66
Cholesterol . . . . 72 milligrams
Total Carbohydrate . . . . 0 grams
   Dietary Fiber . . . . 0 grams
   Sugars . . . . 0 grams
Protein . . . . 26 grams
Sodium . . . . 64 milligrams

BAKED CHICKEN KIEV

6 servings/serving size: 3–4 oz.

This low-fat version of a classic dish is great to serve when entertaining.

- 6 Tbsp. low-calorie margarine
- 3 Tbsp. minced fresh parsley
- 1/2 tsp. dried rosemary
- 1/4 tsp. garlic powder
- Fresh ground pepper

- 3 whole boneless, skinless chicken breasts, halved
- 1/4 cup skim milk
- 1/3 cup fine bread crumbs
- 1 lemon, cut into wedges

1. Combine margarine, parsley, rosemary, garlic and pepper in a small mixing bowl. Shape margarine mixture into six 2-inch long sticks; freeze until firm.
2. Place each chicken breast half between 2 sheets of waxed paper and flatten to 1/4 inch thickness with a meat mallet or rolling pin.
3. Place 1 margarine stick in the center of each chicken breast; fold ends over margarine and roll up, beginning with long side. Secure each end with wooden toothpicks.
4. Dip chicken rolls into the milk and coat thoroughly with bread crumbs. Bake at 400 degrees for 25 minutes until browned.
5. Arrange chicken on a serving platter, spoon juices from pan over the top, garnish with lemon wedges and serve.

....

Lean Meat Exchange 4	Total Carbohydrate . . . . 5 grams
Calories 219	Dietary Fiber . . . . 0 grams
Total Fat . . . . 9 grams	Sugars . . . . 1 gram
Saturated Fat . . . . 2 grams	Protein . . . . 28 grams
Calories from fat 81	Sodium . . . . 210 milligrams
Cholesterol . . . . 73 milligrams	

CHICKEN DIJON

8 servings/serving size: 3–4 oz.

*A*dd *colorful vegetables and wild rice for a complete meal.*

- **4 whole boneless, skinless chicken breasts, halved**
- **1 Tbsp. olive oil**
- **1/4 cup minced onion**
- **2 cups sliced fresh mushrooms**
- **2 garlic cloves, minced**
- **1/2 cup low-sodium chicken broth**
- **1/4 cup dry white wine**
- **Fresh ground pepper**
- **4 Tbsp. minced fresh parsley**
- **1 Tbsp. dijon mustard**

1. Place chicken breasts between 2 sheets of waxed paper; flatten to 1/4 inch using a meat mallet. Coat a large skillet with nonstick cooking spray and place over medium high heat; heat until hot.
2. Add chicken to the skillet and cook for 2 to 3 minutes until chicken is browned on each side. Remove chicken from skillet; set aside and keep warm.
3. In the same pan, add the olive oil. Saute the onion, mushrooms and garlic for 2 to 3 minutes. Add the wine, chicken broth and 2 Tbsp. of the parsley and cook for 3 to 4 minutes.
4. Add the chicken back to the pan and cook over medium heat for 10 to 12 minutes. Remove chicken and vegetables using a slotted spoon. Arrange the chicken on a serving platter and keep warm.
5. Continue cooking broth mixture until it is reduced to 1/3 cup. Remove from heat; whisk in the remaining parsley and mustard. Spoon sauce over the chicken and serve.

....

Lean Meat Exchange 3
Calories 173
Total Fat . . . . 5 grams
   Saturated Fat . . . . 1 gram
   Calories from fat 45
Cholesterol . . . . 72 milligrams

Total Carbohydrate . . . . 2 grams
   Dietary Fiber . . . . 1 gram
   Sugars . . . . 1 gram
Protein . . . . 27 grams
Sodium . . . . 93 milligrams

BAKED CHICKEN WITH WINE SAUCE

8 servings/serving size: 3–4 oz. with sauce

*T*his wine sauce is also delicious with turkey or Cornish game hens.

- 4 whole boneless, skinless chicken breasts, halved
- 4 Tbsp. low-calorie margarine
- 3 Tbsp. flour
- 1/2 cup low-sodium chicken broth
- 3/4 cup low-fat sour cream
- 1/4 cup dry white wine
- 2 tsp. grated lemon rind
- 1 tsp. salt (optional)
- Fresh ground pepper
- 1 tsp. minced fresh thyme
- 1/2 tsp. ground sage
- 1/2 cup sliced mushrooms
- Fresh parsley sprigs

1. Melt 2 Tbsp. of the margarine in a shallow baking dish; place chicken breasts in the dish. Bake in a 350-degree oven, uncovered, for 30 minutes.
2. Meanwhile, melt remaining margarine in a saucepan, add the flour and stir until smooth. Add the chicken broth and stir until mixture is thickened. Add the sour cream, wine, lemon rind, salt, pepper, thyme and sage. Stir until completely smooth.
3. Remove the chicken from the oven and turn the chicken breasts over. Cover the chicken with the mushrooms and pour the sauce over the top. Continue to bake, uncovered, for another 30 minutes or until chicken is tender. Transfer chicken to serving platter, spoon sauce over the chicken, garnish with parsley sprigs and serve.

....

Lean Meat Exchange	3	Cholesterol	72 milligrams
Starch/Bread Exchange	1/2	Total Carbohydrate	6 grams
Calories	214	Dietary Fiber	0 grams
Total Fat	7 grams	Sugars	3 grams
Saturated Fat	2 grams	Protein	29 grams
Calories from fat	67	Sodium	142 milligrams

CHICKEN PROVENCAL

4 servings/serving size: 3–4 oz.

Your guests will love this fast, easy-to-prepare dish.

- ◆ 2 Tbsp. olive oil
- ◆ 1 tsp. dried basil
- ◆ 2 whole boneless, skinless chicken breasts, halved
- ◆ 1 medium garlic clove, minced
- ◆ 1/4 cup minced onion

- ◆ 1/4 cup minced green pepper
- ◆ 1/2 cup dry white wine
- ◆ 1 8-oz. can tomatoes, chopped
- ◆ 1/4 cup pitted black olives
- ◆ Fresh ground pepper

1. Heat the oil in a skillet over medium heat. Stir in basil, add chicken and brown about 3 to 5 minutes.
2. Add the remaining ingredients and cook uncovered over medium heat for 20 minutes or until chicken is tender. Transfer to serving platter and season with additional pepper before serving.

Lean Meat Exchange	4	Cholesterol	72 milligrams
Vegetable Exchange	1	Total Carbohydrate	5 grams
Calories	240	Dietary Fiber	1 gram
Total Fat	11 grams	Sugars	4 grams
Saturated Fat	2 grams	Protein	27 grams
Calories from fat	98	Sodium	294 milligrams

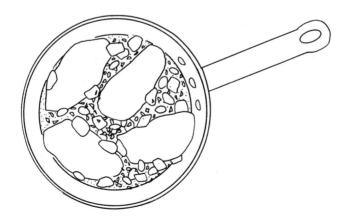

CHICKEN ROSE MARIE

6 servings/serving size: 3–4 oz.

*T*ry serving this dish with orzo (a rice-shaped pasta) and good, crusty
French bread.

- 3 whole boneless, skinless chicken breasts, halved
- 1 cup dried bread crumbs
- 1/4 cup olive oil
- 1/4 cup low-sodium chicken broth
- Grated zest of 1 lemon*
- 3 medium garlic cloves, minced
- 1/4 cup minced fresh parsley
- 1/2 cup fresh lemon juice
- 1/2 cup water
- 1/2 tsp. dried oregano
- 1 medium lemon, cut into wedges
- Parsley sprigs

1. Rinse the chicken in cold water and then roll it in bread crumbs. Spray a skillet with nonstick cooking spray and brown the coated chicken breasts over medium heat about 3 minutes on each side. Transfer the browned chicken to a baking dish.
2. In a small bowl, combine the remaining ingredients, except garnish. Pour the sauce over the chicken. Bake the chicken at 325 degrees, uncovered, for 30 minutes until tender.
3. Transfer to a serving platter and spoon sauce over the chicken. Garnish with lemon and parsley.

....

Lean Meat Exchange	4	Cholesterol	72 milligrams
Starch/Bread Exchange	1	Total Carbohydrate	15 grams
Calories	300	Dietary Fiber	1 gram
Total Fat	13 grams	Sugars	3 grams
Saturated Fat	2 grams	Protein	29 grams
Calories from fat	118	Sodium	225 milligrams

* Obtain lemon zest by grating the rind and inner white part together. Slice the lemon in half, turn sideways and grate. You might want to buy a zester at a cooking store to make this easier!

CHICKEN WITH ALMOND DUXELLES

8 servings/serving size: 3–4 oz.

*T*ucked away inside these moist chicken breasts is a surprising, crunchy filling of almonds, mushrooms and shallots.

- 1/4 cup olive oil
- 1/4 cup dry sherry
- 3/4 pound diced fresh mushrooms
- 4 medium shallots, finely minced
- 2 garlic cloves, minced
- 1 tsp. minced fresh thyme
- Dash cayenne pepper
- 1/2 cup ground almonds
- Dash salt and pepper
- 4 whole boneless, skinless chicken breasts, halved
- Paprika
- 1/2 cup low-fat sour cream

1. In a large skillet over medium heat, heat the olive oil and sherry. Add the mushrooms, shallots, garlic, thyme and cayenne pepper. Cook, stirring often, until mushrooms turn dark.
2. Add the ground almonds, salt and pepper and saute for 2 to 3 minutes. Divide the mixture into 8 portions and place each portion in the center of each chicken breast half. Fold over edges, roll up and place in a baking dish, seam side down, 1 inch apart.
3. Place about 1 Tbsp. of sour cream over each chicken roll and sprinkle with paprika. Bake at 350 degrees for 25 to 30 minutes or until chicken is tender. Transfer to a serving platter and serve.

Lean Meat Exchange	4	Cholesterol	72 milligrams
Starch/Bread Exchange	1/2	Total Carbohydrate	6 grams
Calories	262	Dietary Fiber	1 gram
Total Fat	13 grams	Sugars	5 grams
Saturated Fat	3 grams	Protein	29 grams
Calories from fat	117	Sodium	101 milligrams

CHICKEN WITH GREEN PEPPERCORN SAUCE

4 servings/serving size: 3–4 oz.

This is a quick dish to fix when unexpected guests drop by.

- ◆ 2 Tbsp. olive oil
- ◆ 2 whole boneless, skinless chicken breasts, halved
- ◆ 2 scallions, sliced
- ◆ 1 Tbsp. flour
- ◆ 1/2 cup half-and-half

- ◆ 1/4 cup low-sodium chicken broth
- ◆ 1 tsp. green peppercorns, drained
- ◆ 1/2 tsp. salt (optional)
- ◆ 1/4 cup dry white wine

1. In a large skillet, heat the olive oil over medium heat. Saute chicken for 5 minutes per side; remove to a platter.
2. Saute onions for 1 minute and add the flour. Add the half-and-half, chicken broth, peppercorns and salt. Continue cooking until sauce thickens.
3. Stir in the wine and return the chicken to the pan. Continue cooking until chicken is cooked through. Transfer chicken to a platter and serve with sauce.

....

Lean Meat Exchange 4	Total Carbohydrate . . . . 3 grams
Fat Exchange 1/2	Dietary Fiber . . . . 0 grams
Calories 255	Sugars . . . . 2 grams
Total Fat . . . . 13 grams	Protein . . . . 28 grams
Saturated Fat . . . . 4 grams	Sodium . . . . 346 milligrams
Calories from fat 120	w/o added salt . . . . . . 80 milligrams
Cholesterol . . . . 83 milligrams	

SAUTEED CHICKEN WITH ARTICHOKE HEARTS

6 servings/serving size: 3–4 oz. chicken with topping

*F*resh tarragon is best with this chicken and artichoke flavor combination!

- 3 whole boneless, skinless chicken breasts, halved
- 1/2 cup low-sodium chicken broth
- 1/4 cup dry white wine
- 2 8-oz. cans artichokes, packed in water, drained and quartered
- 1 medium onion, diced
- 1 medium green pepper, chopped
- 1 tsp. minced fresh tarragon (or 1/2 tsp. dried)
- 1/4 tsp. white pepper
- 2 tsp. cornstarch
- 1 Tbsp. cold water
- 2 medium tomatoes, cut into wedges

1. Coat a large skillet with nonstick cooking spray; place over medium heat until hot. Add the chicken and saute until lightly browned, about 3 to 4 minutes per side.
2. Add the chicken broth, wine, artichokes, onion, pepper, tarragon and white pepper; stir well. Bring to a boil, cover, reduce heat and let simmer for 10 to 15 minutes or until chicken and vegetables are tender.
3. Combine the cornstarch and water; add to chicken mixture along with the tomato wedges, stirring until mixture has thickened. Remove from the heat and serve.

....

Lean Meat Exchange 3	Cholesterol . . . . 73 milligrams
Vegetable Exchange 1	Total Carbohydrate . . . . 9 grams
Calories 186	Dietary Fiber . . . . 2 grams
Total Fat . . . . 4 grams	Sugars . . . . 3 grams
Saturated Fat . . . . 1 gram	Protein . . . . 29 grams
Calories from fat 8	Sodium . . . . 250 milligrams

GRILLED CHICKEN WITH GARLIC

4 servings/serving size: 3–4 oz.

Roasted garlic is the secret to this flavorful chicken dish.

- ♦ **2 whole boneless, skinless chicken breasts, halved**
- ♦ **2-1/2 cups red wine**
- ♦ **3 sprigs thyme**
- ♦ **10 garlic cloves, minced**
- ♦ **1/4 cup olive oil**
- ♦ **Fresh ground pepper**

1. In a medium baking dish, combine chicken, red wine, thyme and half of the minced garlic. Marinate for 2 to 3 hours in the refrigerator.
2. Spread remaining cloves of garlic evenly across bottom of a small baking dish, cover with olive oil, and sprinkle with pepper. Bake garlic mixture in a 300-degree oven for 1-1/2 hours or until garlic is tender.
3. Place garlic mixture in a food processor or blender and puree. Remove chicken from marinade.
4. Grill chicken for 10 to 15 minutes, turning frequently and brushing with pureed garlic. Transfer to a platter and serve hot.

....

Lean Meat Exchange	4	Cholesterol	72 milligrams
Fat Exchange	1	Total Carbohydrate	2 grams
Calories	276	Dietary Fiber	0 grams
Total Fat	16 grams	Sugars	2 grams
Saturated Fat	3 grams	Protein	27 grams
Calories from fat	149	Sodium	65 milligrams

GRILLED LEMON MUSTARD CHICKEN

6 servings/serving size: 3 oz.

Note that you need to let the chicken marinate overnight in this recipe!

- **Juice of 6 medium lemons**
- **1/2 cup mustard seeds**
- **1 Tbsp. minced fresh tarragon**
- **2 Tbsp. fresh ground pepper**
- **4 garlic cloves, minced**
- **2 Tbsp. olive oil**
- **3 whole boneless, skinless chicken breasts, halved**

1. In a small mixing bowl, combine the lemon juice, mustard seeds, tarragon, pepper, garlic and oil; mix well.
2. Place chicken in a baking dish and pour marinade on top. Cover and refrigerate overnight.
3. Grill chicken over medium heat for 10 to 15 minutes, basting with marinade. Serve hot.

....

Lean Meat Exchange	3	Total Carbohydrate	2 grams
Calories	167	Dietary Fiber	0 grams
Total Fat	5 grams	Sugars	2 grams
Saturated Fat	1 gram	Protein	27 grams
Calories from fat	47	Sodium	69 milligrams
Cholesterol	72 milligrams		

POACHED CHICKEN WITH BAY LEAVES

8 servings/serving size: 3 oz.

You'll love this poached chicken, surrounded by tender vegetables in a bay leaf-scented broth.

- ◆ 4 quarts low-sodium chicken broth
- ◆ 2 cups dry white wine
- ◆ 4 large bay leaves
- ◆ 4 sprigs fresh thyme
- ◆ Dash salt and pepper
- ◆ 1 4-lb. chicken, giblets removed, washed and patted dry

- ◆ 1/2 lb. carrots, peeled and julienned
- ◆ 1/2 lb. turnips, peeled and julienned
- ◆ 1/2 lb. parsnips, peeled and julienned
- ◆ 4 small leeks, washed and trimmed

1. In a large soup pot, combine broth, wine, bay leaves, thyme, salt and pepper. Let simmer over medium heat while you prepare the chicken.
2. Stuff the cavity with 1/3 each of the carrots, turnips and parsnips, then truss. Add the stuffed chicken to the soup pot and poach, covered, over low heat for 30 minutes.
3. Add remaining vegetables with the leeks and continue to simmer for 25 to 30 minutes, or until juices run clear when the chicken is pierced with a fork.
4. Remove chicken and vegetables to a serving platter. Carve the chicken, remove the skin and surround the sliced meat with poached vegetables to serve.

....

Lean Meat Exchange 3
Calories 226
Total Fat . . . . 7 grams
   Saturated Fat . . . . 2 grams
   Calories from fat 62
Cholesterol . . . . 75 milligrams

Total Carbohydrate . . . . 13 grams
   Dietary Fiber . . . . 3 grams
   Sugars . . . . 6 grams
Protein . . . . 26 grams
Sodium . . . . 138 milligrams

HERBED CORNISH HENS

8 servings/serving size: 4 oz.

A perfect blend of herbs and wine complement the natural flavor of Cornish game hens.

- ♦ **4 Cornish hens**
- ♦ **2 cups light rose wine**
- ♦ **2 garlic cloves, minced**
- ♦ **1/2 tsp. onion powder**
- ♦ **1/2 tsp. celery seeds**
- ♦ **1/2 tsp. poultry seasoning**
- ♦ **1/2 tsp. paprika**
- ♦ **1/2 tsp. basil**
- ♦ **Fresh ground pepper**

1. Remove the giblets from the hens; rinse under cold water and pat dry. Using a long, sharp knife, split each hen lengthwise. You may also buy precut hens.
2. Place the hens, cavity side up, on a rack in a shallow roasting pan. Pour 1-1/2 cups of the wine over the hens; set aside.
3. In a shallow bowl, combine the garlic, onion powder, celery seeds, poultry seasoning, paprika, basil and pepper. Sprinkle half the combined seasonings over the cavity of each split half. Cover and refrigerate. Allow the hens to marinate for 2 to 3 hours.
4. Bake the hens uncovered at 350 degrees for 1 hour. Remove from oven, turn breast side up, pour remaining 1/2 cup wine over the top, and sprinkle with remaining seasonings.
5. Continue to bake for an additional 25 to 30 minutes, basting every 10 minutes until hens are done. Transfer to a serving platter and serve hot.

....

Lean Meat Exchange 4	Total Carbohydrate . . . . 0 grams
Calories 225	Dietary Fiber . . . . 0 grams
Total Fat . . . . 9 grams	Sugars . . . . 0 grams
Saturated Fat . . . . 2 grams	Protein . . . . 34 grams
Calories from fat 78	Sodium . . . . 103 milligrams
Cholesterol . . . . 103 milligrams	

APPLE-GLAZED CORNISH HENS

8 servings/serving size: 4 oz.

*T*his is a great dish to prepare during the holiday season as an alternative to turkey.

- **4 Cornish hens**
- **12 oz. unsweetened apple juice concentrate, undiluted**
- **3 Tbsp. water**
- **1 Tbsp. cornstarch**
- **1 tsp. cinnamon**
- **1 medium lemon, sliced**

1. Remove giblets from hens and discard. Rinse hens under cold water and pat dry. Using a long, sharp knife, split the hens lengthwise. You may also buy precut hens.
2. Place the hens, cavity side up, in a roasting pan. Dilute 1/2 cup of the apple juice concentrate with the water. Pour juice over the hens. Bake uncovered at 350 degrees for 45 minutes. Turn breast side up.
3. In a small pan over medium heat, combine the remaining apple juice concentrate, cornstarch and cinnamon; mix well. Add 4 lemon slices and continue cooking until thickened.
4. Remove from heat and brush hens with the sauce. Return the hens to the oven and continue to bake for an additional 15 minutes. Transfer the hens to a serving platter and garnish with remaining lemon slices.

....

Lean Meat Exchange 4	Cholesterol . . . . 103 milligrams
Fruit Exchange 1/2	Total Carbohydrate . . . . 5 grams
Calories 241	Dietary Fiber . . . . 0 grams
Total Fat . . . . 9 grams	Sugars . . . . 4 grams
Saturated Fat . . . . 2 grams	Protein . . . . 34 grams
Calories from fat 78	Sodium . . . . 106 milligrams

PERFECT PASTA

MAKING PERFECT PASTA

There are at least 150 varieties of pasta to choose from; with the right sauce, pasta is a healthy, low-fat food. Pasta has only about 210 calories per cooked cup and is a good source of complex carbohydrates and B vitamins. Here are a few tips to insure perfect pasta-making all the time.

♦ To cook pasta, start by bringing a cold pot of water to a full rolling boil; this ensures that the pasta cooks properly. Cook pasta to the al dente stage: tender, but still slightly chewy.

♦ Rinse the pasta with cool water to remove the surface starch if you desire, but the starch that clings to the pasta actually helps sauces adhere better.

♦ Cooked pasta lasts for a week in the refrigerator if placed in a covered container; dry pasta in the box will last in your cupboard for a year. Do not freeze cooked pasta, except in casseroles like lasagna.

LINGUINE WITH GARLIC BROCCOLI SAUCE

8 servings/serving size: 1 cup

*W*hite wine adds a special touch to this pasta dish.

- ◆ 3 Tbsp. olive oil
- ◆ 8 medium garlic cloves, minced
- ◆ Fresh ground pepper
- ◆ 1/4 cup dry white wine
- ◆ 1 tsp. dried oregano
- ◆ 1 tsp. dried basil
- ◆ 1/2 tsp. dried thyme
- ◆ 2 cups broccoli florets
- ◆ 2 Tbsp. pine nuts, toasted
- ◆ 1 lb. uncooked linguine
- ◆ 1/4 cup grated Parmesan cheese

1. In a medium skillet over medium heat, heat the oil. Add the garlic and pepper, sauteing for 5 minutes. Add the wine and bring to a boil. Reduce the heat and simmer for 3 to 4 minutes. Add the oregano, basil and thyme.
2. In a large pot of boiling water, add the broccoli florets and then turn off the heat. Immediately rinse the broccoli under cold running water to stop the cooking process. (This method of blanching helps the broccoli to retain its bright green color and crispness.) Add the broccoli to the wine sauce and heat 2 more minutes.
3. Prepare the linguine according to package directions (without adding salt) and drain. Transfer the linguine to a large serving bowl and pour the wine sauce over the top. Sprinkle with Parmesan cheese to serve.

Starch/Bread Exchange 3
Fat Exchange 1
Calories 293
Total Fat . . . . 8 grams
   Saturated Fat . . . . 1 grams
   Calories from fat 73
Cholesterol . . . . 2 milligrams
Total Carbohydrate . . . . 45 grams
   Dietary Fiber . . . . 2 grams
   Sugars . . . . 4 grams
Protein . . . . 10 grams
Sodium . . . . 58 milligrams

LINGUINE WITH CLAM SAUCE

4 servings/serving size: 4 oz. sauce with 1/2 cup linguine

*T*ry this good red clam sauce recipe with other types of pasta or over rice.

- 1/2 cup finely chopped onion
- 1/2 cup finely chopped celery
- 3 medium garlic cloves, minced
- 7 oz. canned clams, minced and drained, reserve juice
- 15 oz. canned whole tomatoes, undrained and chopped
- 1/2 tsp. dried basil
- 1/4 tsp. dried oregano
- 1/2 tsp. hot pepper sauce (Tabasco)
- 1/3 cup finely minced parsley
- 2 cups cooked linguine, hot

1. Coat a large saucepan with nonstick cooking spray; place over medium heat until hot. Saute the onion, celery and garlic until tender.
2. Add reserved clam juice, tomatoes, basil, oregano, and hot pepper sauce to saucepan. Bring to a boil; reduce heat and let simmer, uncovered, for 35 minutes.
3. Stir in clams and parsley; let simmer for 15 to 20 minutes, or until heated through. Place linguine on a platter, spoon sauce over the pasta and serve.

....

Vegetable Exchange 2	Cholesterol . . . . 15 milligrams
Starch/Bread Exchange 1-1/2	Total Carbohydrate . . . . 29 grams
Calories 170	Dietary Fiber . . . . 3 grams
Total Fat . . . . 1 gram	Sugars . . . . 7 grams
Saturated Fat . . . . 0 grams	Protein . . . . 11 grams
Calories from fat 12	Sodium . . . . 287 milligrams

SPAGHETTI WITH PESTO SAUCE

8 servings/serving size: 1 cup pasta plus sauce

*F*resh basil, garlic, cheese and pine nuts turn everyday spaghetti into something special.

- ◆ **3 cups fresh basil, stems removed**
- ◆ **3 garlic cloves, chopped**
- ◆ **1/4 cup olive oil**
- ◆ **3/4 cup pine nuts, toasted**
- ◆ **1/4 cup grated Parmesan cheese**
- ◆ **Fresh ground pepper**
- ◆ **1 lb. cooked spaghetti, hot**

Wash and dry basil. Place basil in a blender or food processor with garlic, olive oil, pine nuts, cheese and pepper; puree. Transfer cooked spaghetti to a serving bowl. Add pesto and toss thoroughly to serve.

Fat Exchange	2-1/2	Cholesterol	2 milligrams
Starch/Bread Exchange	2-1/2	Total Carbohydrate	35 grams
Calories	313	Dietary Fiber	3 grams
Total Fat	16 grams	Sugars	2 grams
Saturated Fat	3 grams	Protein	10 grams
Calories from fat	144	Sodium	50 milligrams

FETTUCINE WITH PEPPERS AND BROCCOLI*

4 servings/serving size: 1 cup

*T*his light pasta entree is loaded with Vitamin C-rich vegetables.

- ◆ **2 Tbsp. olive oil**
- ◆ **2 medium garlic cloves, minced**
- ◆ **2 large red bell peppers, halved, seeded and cut into 1/2-inch strips**

- ◆ **8 oz. uncooked fettucine**
- ◆ **1-1/2 lb. fresh broccoli**
- ◆ **1/4 cup grated Parmesan cheese**

1. In a large skillet over medium heat, heat the olive oil. Add the garlic and saute for 1 minute. Add the peppers and continue sauteing for 3 to 5 minutes or until peppers are just tender, stirring occasionally. Remove from heat and set aside.
2. Prepare the fettucine according to package directions (without adding salt) and drain. Wash the broccoli and peel the tough stalks (if necessary). Steam broccoli for 5 to 6 minutes until it is bright green and retains some crispness. Remove from the heat and set aside.
3. In a large bowl, toss the fettucine with the peppers and arrange the broccoli on top. Sprinkle with Parmesan cheese and serve.

. . . .

Starch/Bread Exchange	3	Cholesterol	58 milligrams
Vegetable Exchange	2	Total Carbohydrate	51 grams
Fat Exchange	1-1/2	Dietary Fiber	7 grams
Calories	362	Sugars	6 grams
Total Fat	11 grams	Protein	15 grams
Saturated Fat	2 grams	Sodium	142 milligrams
Calories from fat	102		

* If the fettucine is made without egg (some is; some isn't), the cholesterol count is zero.

GARLIC FETTUCINE*

5 servings/serving size: 1 cup

This is a great dish for garlic lovers!

- ◆ 2 Tbsp. olive oil
- ◆ 12 plum tomatoes, seeded and diced
- ◆ 4 cloves garlic, minced
- ◆ 1/4 tsp. salt (optional)
- ◆ Fresh ground pepper

- ◆ 1 tsp. capers
- ◆ 2 tsp. chopped black olives
- ◆ 6 oz. uncooked fettucine
- ◆ 1/4 cup chopped fresh basil
- ◆ Parsley sprigs for garnish

1. In a large saucepan over medium heat, heat the oil. Add the tomatoes, garlic, salt, pepper, capers and olives. Let simmer over low heat for 30 minutes, stirring occasionally.
2. Prepare the fettucine according to package directions (without adding salt) and drain. Transfer the fettucine to a serving bowl and spoon sauce and chopped basil on top. Garnish with parsley sprigs to serve.

....

Starch/Bread Exchange	2	Cholesterol	32 milligrams
Vegetable Exchange	1	Total Carbohydrate	38 grams
Fat Exchange	1	Dietary Fiber	4 grams
Calories	240	Sugars	10 grams
Total Fat	8 grams	Protein	7 grams
Saturated Fat	1 gram	Sodium	147 milligrams
Calories from fat	71	w/o added salt	51 milligrams

* If the fettucine is made without egg (some is; some isn't), the cholesterol count is zero.

PASTA WITH VEGETABLE CLAM SAUCE

8 servings/serving size: 1/2 cup pasta plus sauce

This recipe works best with a shaped pasta like rigatoni or shells, so the vegetables stick to the pasta.

- 5 medium cloves garlic, crushed
- 2 Tbsp. olive oil
- 4 celery stalks, chopped
- 2 small zucchini, thinly sliced
- 4 scallions, chopped
- 1/4 lb. fresh mushrooms, sliced
- 2 Tbsp. chopped fresh parsley
- 7 oz. clams, undrained
- 2 small tomatoes, chopped
- 1/3 cup dry white wine
- 2 Tbsp. fresh lemon juice
- Fresh ground pepper
- 1 lb. cooked, shaped pasta
- Grated Parmesan cheese

1. In a large skillet over medium heat, saute garlic in oil until lightly browned. Add celery, zucchini, scallions, mushrooms and parsley; saute until vegetables are just tender (about 5 minutes).
2. Add clams with their juice, tomatoes, wine and pepper; stir well. Let simmer, uncovered, for 4 to 5 minutes. Place cooked pasta on a serving platter. Remove sauce from heat and spoon over the pasta. Sprinkle with cheese and serve.

....

Starch/Bread Exchange 1	Cholesterol . . . . 10 milligrams
Vegetable Exchange 1	Total Carbohydrate . . . . 22 grams
Fat Exchange 1	Dietary Fiber . . . . 2 grams
Calories 162	Sugars . . . . 5 grams
Total Fat . . . . 5 grams	Protein . . . . 8 grams
Saturated Fat . . . . 1 gram	Sodium . . . . 94 milligrams
Calories from fat 42	

SHRIMP AND PASTA DELIGHT

4 servings/serving size: 1 cup

These large, tender shrimp are delicious in a mushroom tomato sauce.

- 2 Tbsp. olive oil
- 1/2 lb. mushrooms, sliced thinly
- 2 stalks celery, sliced diagonally
- 2 scallions, sliced
- 1/4 cup diced red pepper
- 2 Tbsp. chopped parsley

- 1-1/2 lb. peeled and deveined large shrimp
- 3 Tbsp. fresh lemon juice
- 6 plum tomatoes, diced
- 1 tsp. capers
- Fresh ground pepper
- 8 oz. cooked vermicelli noodles, kept hot

1. In a large skillet over medium heat, heat the olive oil. Add the mushrooms, celery, scallions, red pepper and parsley; cover and let simmer over low heat for 8 minutes, stirring occasionally.

2. Add the shrimp and lemon juice to the pan and cook until the shrimp just turn bright pink (about 3 to 4 minutes). Add the tomatoes, capers and pepper and cook for 1 to 2 minutes more.

3. Mound the cooked, hot vermicelli on a platter and spoon shrimp mixture over top to serve.

Lean Meat Exchange 3	Cholesterol . . . . 197 milligrams
Vegetable Exchange 1	Total Carbohydrate . . . . 28 grams
Starch/Bread Exchange 1	Dietary Fiber . . . . 4 grams
Calories 294	Sugars . . . . 7 grams
Total Fat . . . . 9 grams	Protein . . . . 26 grams
Saturated Fat . . . . 1 gram	Sodium . . . . 264 milligrams
Calories from fat 82	

RIGATONI WITH CHICKEN AND THREE PEPPER SAUCE

8 servings/serving size: 1/2 chicken breast
with pepper sauce and 1 cup pasta

*T*his dish is slightly spicy and very colorful!

- 16 oz. uncooked rigatoni (or substitute any other shaped pasta)
- 1/4 cup olive oil
- 1 medium onion, chopped
- 1 large green pepper, julienned
- 1 large red pepper, julienned
- 1 large yellow pepper, julienned
- 2 garlic cloves, minced

- 2 tomatoes, chopped
- 1/2 cup low-sodium chicken broth
- 1/4 cup minced parsley
- 1/2 tsp. dried basil
- Dash salt and pepper (optional)
- Dash crushed red pepper
- 2 Tbsp. lemon juice
- 4 boneless, skinless chicken breasts, halved and cooked

1. Cook the rigatoni according to package directions (without adding salt), drain and set aside. In a large skillet, over medium heat, heat the oil. Add the onion, peppers and garlic and saute for 6 minutes.

2. Add the tomatoes, chicken broth, parsley, basil, salt, pepper and crushed red pepper. Add lemon juice. Add chicken to the skillet and cook chicken in sauce over low heat just until chicken is warmed in the sauce.

3. Arrange the cooked rigatoni on a serving platter. Spoon chicken and pepper sauce over rigatoni and serve.

Lean Meat Exchange	3	Cholesterol	72 milligrams
Starch/Bread Exchange	3	Total Carbohydrate	50 grams
Vegetable Exchange	1	Dietary Fiber	3 grams
Calories	448	Sugars	6 grams
Total Fat	11 grams	Protein	35 grams
Saturated Fat	2 grams	Sodium	94 milligrams
Calories from fat	100	w/o added salt	78 milligrams

CHEESY EGGPLANT CASSEROLE*

6 servings/serving size: 1 cup

- 1-3/4 cup chopped onion
- 2 medium garlic cloves, minced
- 16 oz. whole tomatoes, undrained
- 1/4 cup tomato paste
- 2 Tbsp. chopped fresh parsley
- 1 tsp. oregano
- 1/2 tsp. dried basil
- Fresh ground pepper
- 1 large eggplant, peeled and sliced into 1/4-inch slices
- 1 cup shredded nonfat mozzarella cheese
- 1 cup low-fat cottage cheese
- 4 Tbsp. grated Parmesan cheese

1. Coat a large skillet with nonstick cooking spray. Add the onion and garlic to the skillet and saute over low heat until onion is tender (about 6 minutes).
2. Stir in undrained whole tomatoes, tomato paste, parsley, salt, oregano, basil, and pepper. Bring mixture to a boil; reduce heat and let simmer, uncovered, for 40 to 50 minutes, stirring occasionally.
3. Arrange eggplant slices on a steamer rack, place in a large pot to which 1 inch of water has been added, and steam for about 5 minutes until eggplant is tender. Do not overcook. Combine the mozzarella and cottage cheeses together and set aside.
4. Coat a 13x9x2-inch baking pan with nonstick cooking spray and place a layer of eggplant in the pan. Top eggplant with some of the sauce mixture and some of the cheese mixture and sprinkle with Parmesan cheese. Repeat the steps in layers until all the ingredients are used.
5. Bake at 350 degrees for 30 to 35 minutes and serve hot.

•••

Medium-Fat Meat Exchange 1	Cholesterol .... 19 milligrams
Starch/Bread Exchange 1	Total Carbohydrate .... 18 grams
Vegetable Exchange 1	Dietary Fiber .... 3 grams
Calories 177	Sugars .... 11 grams
Total Fat .... 6 grams	Protein .... 15 grams
Saturated Fat .... 4 grams	Sodium .... 546 milligrams
Calories from fat 54	

* This dish is relatively high in sodium!

BOUNTIFUL BRUNCHES

FRUIT PUFF PANCAKE

4 servings/serving size: 1/4 recipe

- **5 egg substitute equivalents**
- **1/2 cup skim milk**
- **1/2 cup flour**
- **1 Tbsp. vanilla extract**

- **4 cups mixed fresh fruit** (try sliced strawberries, blueberries, and bananas)

1. Preheat the oven to 425 degrees. Spray a pie plate or oven-proof skillet with nonstick cooking spray. In a large bowl, combine the eggs and milk. Add the flour and vanilla.
2. Pour the batter into the prepared pan and place it in the oven. Bake for 15 to 20 minutes until batter is puffed and edges are browned. Remove the puff pancake, fill the center with the fruit, cut into wedges and serve.

Starch/Bread Exchange	1-1/2	Cholesterol	1 milligram
Fruit Exchange	1	Total Carbohydrate	36 grams
Calories	184	Dietary Fiber	4 grams
Total Fat	1 gram	Sugars	16 grams
Saturated Fat	0 grams	Protein	10 grams
Calories from fat	7	Sodium	120 milligrams

ITALIAN FRITTATA

4 servings/serving size: 1/4 recipe

You can serve this open-faced egg dish for casual breakfasts, too.

- **1/2 tsp. olive oil**
- **5 egg substitute equivalents**
- **2 cups mixed steamed vegetables** (try chopped broccoli, asparagus, and red peppers)
- **2 tsp. minced garlic**
- **2 Tbsp. minced chives**
- **1 tsp. dried oregano**
- **1 tsp. dried basil**
- **Fresh ground pepper**
- **1/4 cup fresh grated Parmesan cheese**

1. Add the oil to an oven-proof skillet or pie plate. In a large bowl, combine the remaining ingredients and add to the skillet.
2. Set the skillet in the oven and bake the frittata for 14 to 17 minutes until set. Remove from the oven and loosen edges with a spatula. Sprinkle with grated cheese, cut into wedges and serve.

....

Lean Meat Exchange	1	Cholesterol	4 milligrams
Vegetable Exchange	1	Total Carbohydrate	6 grams
Calories	82	Dietary Fiber	3 grams
Total Fat	2 grams	Sugars	3 grams
Saturated Fat	1 gram	Protein	10 grams
Calories from fat	20	Sodium	203 milligrams

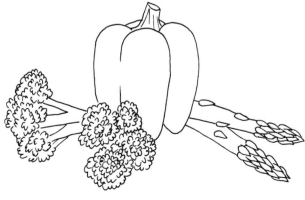

EGG AND WILD RICE OMELET

3 servings/serving size: 1/3 omelet

The surprise of wild rice adds a unique touch to this omelet.

- **8 egg substitute equivalents**
- **1/2 cup skim milk**
- **1 cup cooked wild rice**
- **1/2 tsp. hot pepper sauce (Tabasco)**

- **1-1/2 tsp. Worcestershire sauce**
- **1 Tbsp. chopped fresh parsley**

1. In a medium bowl, combine all the ingredients except for the parsley. Beat mixture thoroughly.
2. Coat a large nonstick skillet with cooking spray and place over medium heat until hot. Pour egg mixture into skillet. As eggs begin to cook, gently lift sides of omelet and tilt pan to allow uncooked portions of the egg to flow underneath.
3. Cook until eggs are set but still moist, sprinkle top with chopped parsley and transfer to a serving platter. Serve hot.

....

Lean Meat Exchange 1	Cholesterol . . . . 1 milligram
Starch/Bread Exchange 1	Total Carbohydrate . . . . 17 grams
Calories 139	Dietary Fiber . . . . 1 gram
Total Fat . . . . 0 grams	Sugars . . . . 5 grams
Saturated Fat . . . . 0 grams	Protein . . . . 17 grams
Calories from fat 0	Sodium . . . . 262 milligrams

SHRIMP OMELET

4 servings/serving size: 1/4 omelet

*Y*ou can cut this open-faced omelet into wedges for brunch or smaller squares for an appetizer.

- ◆ **5 egg substitute equivalents**
- ◆ **1 Tbsp. lite soy sauce**
- ◆ **1/2 cup chopped onions**
- ◆ **2 Tbsp. low-calorie margarine**

- ◆ **1/2 cup minced fresh shrimp (about 4–5 shrimp, shelled, deveined, and cooked)**

1. In a small bowl, beat eggs and soy sauce thoroughly; add the onions. In a skillet over low heat, melt the margarine until just hot.
2. Pour half of the egg mixture into the skillet, spread shrimp over the top, and add the remaining egg mixture. Continue to cook until the eggs are set, transfer to a serving plate, cut into wedges and serve.

....

Medium-Fat Meat Exchange 1	Total Carbohydrate . . . . 4 grams
Calories 81	Dietary Fiber . . . . 0 grams
Total Fat . . . . 3 grams	Sugars . . . . 3 grams
Saturated Fat . . . . 1 gram	Protein . . . . 10 grams
Calories from fat 27	Sodium . . . . 328 milligrams
Cholesterol . . . . 28 milligrams	

DEVILED CRAB

6 servings/serving size: 1 ramekin

*T*ry serving a light, refreshing tomato and cucumber salad with this dish.

- 1 tsp. low-calorie margarine
- 1 cup chopped celery
- 1/2 cup chopped onion
- 1 cup diced whole wheat bread
- 1 tsp. dried thyme
- 3 Tbsp. chopped fresh parsley
- 2 Tbsp. dry sherry
- 1 lb. fresh crab meat, drained and flaked
- 1 egg substitute, slightly beaten
- Fresh ground pepper

1. Preheat the oven to 350 degrees. Coat a large skillet with nonstick cooking spray; add margarine and place over medium heat until margarine melts.
2. Add celery and onion and saute for 5 minutes. Remove from heat, stir in remaining ingredients and mix thoroughly.
3. Coat 6 ramekins or custard cups with nonstick cooking spray. Divide mixture evenly into each cup and bake for 20 to 25 minutes. Serve hot.

....

Lean Meat Exchange	1	Cholesterol	65 milligrams
Starch/Bread Exchange	1/2	Total Carbohydrate	7 grams
Calories	109	Dietary Fiber	1 gram
Total Fat	2 grams	Sugars	2 grams
Saturated Fat	0 grams	Protein	15 grams
Calories from fat	17	Sodium	264 milligrams

CRUSTLESS ARTICHOKE QUICHE

8 servings/serving size: 1/8 pie

*S*ave unwanted calories and fat by serving this cheesy crustless quiche.

- 14 oz. canned artichoke hearts, packed in water
- 1 Tbsp. low-calorie margarine
- 1/4 lb. fresh mushrooms
- 2 cups shredded Muenster cheese
- 4 egg substitute equivalents
- 1 cup skim milk
- 1/4 tsp. dried basil
- Fresh ground pepper
- Paprika

1. Preheat the oven to 350 degrees. Drain and chop artichokes; place on paper towels and squeeze dry.
2. Coat a 9-inch quiche dish or pie plate with nonstick cooking spray. Arrange the artichokes in quiche dish and set aside.
3. In a small skillet, saute the mushrooms in margarine until tender; drain and place in quiche dish. Sprinkle cheese evenly over the top.
4. In a small bowl, combine the eggs, skim milk, basil, and pepper; mix well. Pour egg mixture over cheese and sprinkle with paprika. Bake for 40 to 50 minutes or until center is firm. Remove from oven and serve hot.

· ·

Medium-Fat Meat Exchange	1	Cholesterol	28 milligrams
Vegetable Exchange	1	Total Carbohydrate	4 grams
Fat Exchange	1	Dietary Fiber	1 gram
Calories	145	Sugars	2 grams
Total Fat	10 grams	Protein	12 grams
Saturated Fat	6 grams	Sodium	338 milligrams
Calories from fat	86		

MINI BREAKFAST QUICHES

12 servings/serving size: 1 muffin cup

*Y*ou can also serve these mini quiches as an appetizer.

- ◆ **4 oz. diced green chilies**
- ◆ **2 oz. diced pimentos, drained**
- ◆ **3 cups precooked white rice**
- ◆ **2 egg substitute equivalents**

- ◆ **1/3 cup skim milk**
- ◆ **1/2 tsp. cumin**
- ◆ **Dash salt and pepper**
- ◆ **1 cup low-fat cheddar cheese**

1. Preheat the oven to 400 degrees. In a large mixing bowl, combine the chilies, pimentos, rice, eggs, milk, cumin, salt, pepper and 1/2 cup of the cheese.
2. Spoon mixture evenly into muffin cups and sprinkle with remaining cheese. Bake for 12 to 15 minutes or until set. Carefully remove the quiches from the pan, arrange on a platter and serve.

Starch/Bread Exchange 1
Calories 88
Total Fat .... 2 grams
   Saturated Fat .... 1 gram
   Calories from fat 16
Cholesterol .... 7 milligrams

Total Carbohydrate .... 13 grams
   Dietary Fiber .... 0 grams
   Sugars .... 1 gram
Protein .... 5 grams
Sodium .... 98 milligrams

INDEX

DIG INTO OUR *RECIPE-PACKED PANTRY OF COOKBOOKS AND MENU PLANNERS*

Healthy Selects:
Spark Plugs for Your Taste Buds

Dozens of recipes were chosen for each *Healthy Selects* cookbook, but only the 64 most tempting were chosen. Every recipe will fit nicely into your healthy meal plan. Calories, fats, sodium, carbohydrates, cholesterol counts, and food exchanges accompany every recipe.

♦ **GREAT STARTS & FINE FINISHES**

Now you can begin every dinner with an enticing appetizer and finish it off with a "now I'm REALLY satisfied" dessert. Choose from recipes like Crab-Filled Mushrooms, Broiled Shrimp with Garlic, Baked Scallops, Creamy Tarragon Dip, or Cheesy Tortilla Wedges to start; serve Cherry Cobbler, Fresh Apple Pie, Cherry Cheesecake, Chocolate Cupcakes, or dozens of others to finish. Softcover. #CCBGSFF
Nonmember: $8.95/Member: $7.15

♦ **EASY & ELEGANT ENTREES**

Softcover. #CCBEEE. *Nonmember: $8.95/Member: $7.15*

♦ **SAVORY SOUPS & SALADS**

When your meals need a little something extra, or you just want something light, invite *Savory Soups & Salads* to lunch and dinner. They just might become your favorite guests. Choose from Pasta-Stuffed Tomato Salad, Mediterranean Chicken Salad, Hot Clam Chowder, Cool Gazpacho, and more. Softcover. #CCBSSS
Nonmember: $8.95/Member: $7.15

♦ **QUICK & HEARTY MAIN DISHES**

When you're looking for simple, great-tasting meals but can't quite find the time, it's time for *Quick & Hearty Main Dishes.* You'll find Apple Cinnamon Pork Chops, Beef Stroganoff, Broiled Salmon Steaks, Spicy Chicken Drumsticks, Almond Chicken, and many others. Softcover. #CCBQHMD
Nonmember: $8.95/Member: $7.15

♦ **SIMPLE & TASTY SIDE DISHES**

Add a spark of flavor to your main course from four tasty categories of easy-to-prepare sides. In just minutes you can have Herb-Broiled Tomatoes, Sherried Peppers with Bean Sprouts, Brown Rice with Mushrooms, Zucchini & Carrot Salad, Scalloped Potatoes, and dozens of others keeping company with your favorite entrees. Softcover. #CCBSTSD
Nonmember: $8.95/Member: $7.15

The *Month of Meals* series:
Automatic meal planning with a turn of the page

Each *Month of Meals* menu planner offers 28 days' worth of fresh new menu choices. The pages are split into thirds and interchangeable, so you can flip to any combination of breakfast, lunch, and dinner. So no matter which combinations you choose, your nutrients and exchanges will still be correct for the entire day—automatically!

◆ **MONTH OF MEALS**
Choose from Chicken Cacciatore, Oven Fried Fish, Sloppy Joes, Crab Cakes, many others. Spiral-bound. #CMPMOM
Nonmember: $12.50/Member: $9.95

◆ **MONTH OF MEALS 2**
Month of Meals 2 features tips and meal suggestions for Mexican, Italian, and Chinese restaurants. Menu choices include Beef Burritos, Chop Suey, Veal Piccata, Stuffed Peppers, many others. Spiral-bound. #CMPMOM2
Nonmember: $12.50/Member: $9.95

◆ **MONTH OF MEALS 3**
How long has it been since you could eat fast food without guilt? Now you can—*Month of Meals 3* shows you how. Choose from McDonald's, Wendy's, Taco Bell, and others. Menu choices include Kentucky Fried Chicken, Stouffer's Macaroni and Cheese, Fajita in a Pita, Seafood Stir Fry, others. Spiral-bound. #CMPMOM3
Nonmember: $12.50/Member: $9.95

◆ **MONTH OF MEALS 4**
Beef up your meal planning with our "meat and potatoes" menu planner. Menu options include Oven Crispy Chicken, Beef Stroganoff, Cornbread Pie, many others. Spiral-bound. #CMPMOM4
Nonmember: $12.50/Member: $9.95

◆ **MONTH OF MEALS 5**
Automatic meal planning goes vegetarian! Choose from a garden of fresh selections like Eggplant Italian, Stuffed Zucchini, Cucumbers with Dill Dressing, Vegetable Lasagna, many others. Spiral-bound. #CMPMOM5
Nonmember: $12.50/Member: $9.95

◆ **HEALTHY HOMESTYLE COOKBOOK**
Choose from more than 150 healthy new recipes with old-fashioned great taste. Just like grandma used to make—but **without** all that fat. Complete nutrition information—calories, protein, fat, fiber, saturated fat, sodium, cholesterol, carbohydrate counts and diabetic exchanges—accompanies every recipe. Special introductory section features "how-to" cooking tips, plus energy- and time-saving tips for microwaving. Lay-flat binding allows hands-free reference to any recipe. Softcover. #CCBHHS
Nonmember: $12.50/Member: $9.95

☐ **YES!** Please send me the following books:

Book Name: _____ Quantity: _____
Item Number: _____
Price Each: _____ Total: _____

Book Name: _____ Quantity: _____
Item Number: _____
Price Each: _____ Total: _____

Book Name: _____ Quantity: _____
Item Number: _____
Price Each: _____ Total: _____

Book Name: _____ Quantity: _____
Item Number: _____
Price Each: _____ Total: _____

Publications Subtotal $ _____
Virginia residents add 4.5% state sales tax $ _____
Add shipping & handling (see chart) $ _____
Add $15 for each international shipment $ _____
GRAND TOTAL $ _____

Name _____

Address _____

City/State/Zip _____

☐ Payment enclosed (check or money order)
☐ Charge my: ☐ VISA ☐ MasterCard ☐ American Express

Account Number _____

Signature _____

Exp. Date _____   CHA94HS

Shipping & Handling
Up to $30 . . . . .add $3.00
$30.01-$50 . . . . .add $4.00
Over $50 . . . . .add 8%

Mail to: American Diabetes Association
          1970 Chain Bridge Road
          McLean, VA 22109-0592

Allow 2-3 weeks for shipment. Add $3 for each extra shipping address. Prices subject to change without notice. Foreign orders must be paid in U.S. funds, drawn on a U.S. bank.